Sleep The Enemy

(PTSD) Post Traumatic Stress Disorder

Alfonso Gamble Sr.

outskirts
press

Sleeping with the Enemy (PTSD)

This is another journey from within that author Alfonso Gamble Sr. is going to take his readers on. The author of *Looking At You Finding Myself* and *MIA: Missing in America (Our Sons)* now sits down after some healing and growth from sleeping with this enemy now known as PTSD and takes you on some of his journey with this enemy. My hope is that some readers will come to know this enemy. Being a Vietnam veteran, I will share some of the ways PTSD came into my life in hope that if you are a veteran of any war you will come to know this enemy for yourselves. Not that you have to be veteran of any military wars; you will learn that there are many other ways that you could be one of the many people in this society that sleep with this enemy known as PTSD. So, come with me and let me see if I can help you come face-to-face with this enemy, and see it for what it is and some ways it can get into our bedroom. I pray that you won't be afraid anymore to look under the bed or close your eyes at night, or to talk to your loved ones about this enemy or be around them in your fear of self. From not knowing this enemy that you or even them could be sleeping with, so you won't be too afraid to talk to each other about it. For the fear of anyone knowing your secret they wouldn't love you or want to be around you anymore. This book is also for the many that are being locked away in their home, hospital, and lost from self and life. It's my hope that they will be able to come out and live again with their family and a society that will now know some of their pain. With that hope and seeing some of the many faces that this enemy has PTSD, so that our society won't lose out from lost dreams because I know that we as a people never know which or what dream will take this world and our society to its next level of life. Also to our children's and love ones that need us in their lives.

HEALING

Dedication

This book is dedicated to the veteran men and women who have dealt with this enemy without knowing what it was or what was going on with them. Also, to those who live long enough to aid the doctor with new information so that others won't have to die. Also, to the millions of family and children who need closure from the loss of their loved ones, so that they might know that it wasn't their husband, wives or child, but this enemy (PTSD) that lives from within that kept their loved ones from them. My prayer is that your spouse, or children or loved ones will know that we love them and help for them is on the way.

I also dedicated this book to Vietnam veterans for standing up to our society saying that we won't go away in to the night, leaving behind our brother or their family with those old beliefs that we were shell-shocked, knowing that it was something else. Thank you

Also, I would like to thank the few doctors that believed in us enough to take a stand saying that those old diagnoses were wrong by putting their jobs and career on the line to help us and save many other lives, but more important saving the lives of many of those family member life.

To my family, thank you for hanging in there with your father, from the ones that are close and to those that are far, by letting me be myself and help my grand- and great-grandchildren find love for me after all the pain I put them through. A special thanks to a dear friend that was to this world and myself in February of 2014,Jeanette Ossie Amous; thank you and I love you and will always miss you. Now a special dedication to Bertha Ann Burns, who is now standing with me in this new chapter of my life: I love you and always will. Forgive me for all the abuse you have taken from me, and from others who still don't think that I will make it to the other side after fighting with this enemy some 30 years later.

Life Not Death

Peace

Introduction

Here I am once again with hope and prayers that I have been given some healing information to share with you on another journey from within. This is journey about an enemy that I lived with for many years, and I know that I will receive some more growth and understanding about this enemy that I have come to know as PTSD. Now I pray that you will find some healing and growth so that you won't have to sleep with it as long as I did. Now this book will take you a lot deeper than some of my other work; it will take you to places where many who sleep with this enemy think that there is a boogeyman behind many of our closet doors or that a monster is somewhere waiting on them. So, hold on to your hat because we are going to get to work so that you will find some healing and growth for yourself and your loved ones. This may mean putting up a good fight for others who may be in pain and still sleeping and living with this enemy (PTSD) today.

This enemy comes with a lot of different faces, and many other diagnoses. First and foremost, I need to let you know that some of the pain that comes with this enemy can come from the good, bad, and the ugly. These three things have a lot to do with our mood, feelings, and behavior and there are other areas where this enemy lives with us throughout the day like our mind, body, and spirit; with these three faces it will have us crying, laughing, and running from ourselves. There are other ways this enemy can make us hurt ourselves along with hurting our family members without even touching them; that hurt can come without even picking up a gun or knife. So please let's take this work we are about to do for real and not just something we read about that happens to other families, children, or people. Believe me, many of us sleep with this enemy every night and walk with it every day.

You see, we not only sleep with this enemy at night, but we walk with him in the day too, something we all know as sleepwalking. Those faces can come with depression, anger, and fear. So please don't take this enemy with a grain of salt, or sugar, because when it is good it's bad.

There are other areas we will visit on this journey of sleeping with this enemy; hold on to your seat because this ride will cause some pain, but if you stay with me here there will be healing and growth also.

Being a Vietnam veteran is where I saw PTSD, first from a warrior point of view, now for myself and others; we now see it in many different forms and levels, because trauma is trauma no matter how it came into our lives. This society has many other ways that this enemy that we sleep with can become a part of our lives and many other family members' lives in this world. So, let's be clear on this so we won't let the next person with this diagnosis be locked away from their loved ones. Just because they are sleeping with this enemy and it has separated them from our society to destroy and kill them from within.

I don't know if you have heard or read about PTSD, which is POST-TRAUMATIC STRESS DISORDER, or not but here is the definition I found that you may want to look at. Post means coming after in time, as a rejection of or in reaction in time. Traumatic means bodily injury or shock; psychiatry: a painful emotional experience, lasting trauma, or abnormal condition caused by it. Stress means strain or straining force, force exerted upon a body that tends to strain or deform its shape, mental or physical tension or strain. Disorder - a lack of order, confusion that will upset the normal functions or health. These are just some of the definitions that can be found about PTSD that will hopefully get your wheels turning, so let's not stop here. We can all find the difference in as many ways as we want to, with some of those reasons that people are dying, so please hear me here. Look for the similarity not the difference. For in that moment it took you looking at difference, we lost another human being and it could have been one of your loved ones.

Now before I get to what I believe my journey and GOD have brought me here for in the first place, there is another point of view I am going to tell you about and you might want to visit it from some of your own experience. I know you may have had some of these experience in one way or another. I believe they, too, are a part of this enemy; it's all in how you look at them, or why they come to you. What I am talking about here are nightmares and flashbacks. You do know that these things are just half of the problem and we who sleep with this enemy may go through some nights when we ball up in knots. Do you know that this enemy can be passed down from person to person; this I have come to believe.

The fact is that I myself can see it in some of my children, like the ones who have anger issues or behavior problems, but we as a society won't say that truth until one of our veteran children gets in trouble down the road in their lives, and then we want to say things like "You know his father (or mother) was in the war." If that's the truth, then yes, it can travel around from member to member who sleep in the same house or even in the same bed like our wives. So please take a good look at this enemy before you walk away from that loved one and put them out of your circle of life. It is one thing to be lost from self, but another to be lost to your family, society, and the world.

Now before we get down to work, there is another thing about this enemy I think you should know about: Wounds can arise that are not a flesh wound or body part missing like an arm or a leg; this wound comes from the mind and spirit, so please don't kick a person down because you can't see these wounds. Instead, give them a hand up, not a hand out. When we sit still and let an enemy like this live on from these wounds, we will see things happen within us, now from my time in the Vietnam War. The longer we take to help these soldiers and family members in their lives, the longer they will live with this horror and the more our society will lose. This can be from the White House to the poor house. Many of us don't know about this enemy because of one thing or the other; it could be our knowledge or our society overlooking this problem too long. As the old saying goes, you can pay me now or pay me later.

There is another way to take a close look at this enemy, and that way is from the mental field. This illness is robbing our society of the worthiest things like human life, hope, and happiness. This is something I pray that you won't take lightly because if you do, then you could become one of those I wrote about in my book *MIA: Missing In America (Our Sons)* so please read on and learn as much as you can so that we won't let the enemy, PTSD, take over more light and turn it into darkness. These are just some of the topics we will talk about and you will read about, so on hold on to your seat. Author Alfonso Gamble is about to take you into some of those dark places where people think that the boogeyman or a monster lives. For what I hope with this gift is that you stay alive and have a happy life with your family. Society can't afford to lose one more of GOD's children, if nothing more than just helping them by shining some light in the darkness so that other loved ones won't be lost from the light. With that let's go back and take our home, town, state, and our country back. Along with our world. Are you with me or are you one of those who will say my house is okay; we don't have any people like that in our family? Just take another look if he/she is there, or are you blind to self and don't want to see them? So, don't just put them away and tell yourself out of sight out of mind. Until the time comes when the enemy takes over, leaving you with these words within your mind that our society also is saying after the facts I didn't know. Well, here is a good place and time to learn.

There is one other thing before closing this introduction I would like for you know and that is about 50 percent of our society sleeps with this enemy without ever knowing that there is an enemy within them known as PTSD. Or they just don't want other to know that there is something going on with them out of fear from rejection or losing their job or the title that we hold in our community or in this society,most of all in life.

Leave No One

Behind

Table of Contents

CHAPTER 1

Living in Darkness (unknown)

THERE ARE MANY places I could start with you on this journey. I always said first things first, and living with the enemy, not knowing who or what it was, I had to fight far too long. I guess a good place to start was with me coming back home from my first tour in Vietnam, and that was when just being around people without the madness was too much for me. You see, if there weren't any loud noise or people I could get into a fight with, then something was wrong in my mind and life. How is that possible? Well, I'm glad you asked the question, because here is where the light left and darkness took over in my life, I believe. Let's see if there is a place like this in your life. Now this doesn't have to be something that you get from returning from war; it could be something as small as you seeing something that traumatizes you, anything from a car accident or the loss of a friend one summer day in a drowning accident.

If you find yourself reading along here, looking at the differences instead of the similarities, then you may not see the real problem, and you are right where I was some twenty-five years ago. Right here when things started happening to me and other soldiers, when I began to rule myself out of that group of soldiers with this illness that lived within me. What I didn't know was that this enemy had a name, PTSD. What it wanted me to do was to look for differences not similarities, and it got me alone with just it and the horror that came along with isolation. That was when I found myself lying awake many of those sleepless nights and drinking my way through my days. This wasn't something I wanted to do. What I know today is that I listened to people who didn't know anything about this enemy or believe there was something else going on with me and gave me some negative coping skills. For me that happened long before I returned home and before I got out of the military. When you are with family members and others, you could pass along some of those old coping skills for you to deal with the new enemy. That could cause great harm to you and bring more traumas in your life. First you may have to ask yourself what coping skill was given to you—was it medication or was it street drugs? Or were you told the same things that many others before you were told, that was to get over it, or was you thrown in a dark room all alone to deal with this enemy on your own. Those were some of the first things and ways I was taught and told. Some of those people I thought were my friends and doctor and my lover. What about you?

The first time I found myself feeling alone was when I found myself balled up in a knot in bed not knowing what to do, also not wanting others to know or see the fear on my face of not feeling human. So, what do you think the enemy gave me (darkness) so that I would feel more human and less fearful, of me and the world around me? This was one of my first times hiding from the light (truth) and coming to understand that later in life, that darkness became a way of life for me. Now this went on way too long before I felt right living in a world where there was no killing, and living without looking over my shoulder was a way of life for me. So, I returned to the Vietnam War, which wasn't a safe place to be, but it was a good place to hide out. Also, in that world I could live without having the fear that came with living in the real world back home with family and friends. So, you see here, this is one of my dark places where this enemy became smarter than me; in these dark places it can know you better sometimes than you know yourself. Also, it keeps one step ahead of you in your thinking, action, and behavior. Take some note here if you have to, so that you don't let this enemy get the drop on you and have you looking at the differences not the similarities, and telling yourself that you are not like them.

With all this going on inside of me and being afraid to tell anyone, the next thing it told me was to go back home (Vietnam War), where I could live the way I wanted to without anyone knowing my fears and pain. This is one of the ways we keep our family from learning or knowing about our problem. This was an excuse for me that worked. What did it take for you? Ask yourself without letting the enemy tell you a lie.

Here's another one of those hiding places for me that felt like a rush or a high. I'm talking about racing cars, to go as fast as I could. It was one of my greatest rushes to go faster than anyone else; that way no one would see or know the real fear that I carry within. Not knowing that this enemy, PTSD, really wanted me dead. So for those thirty days on leave I tried to buy the fastest car I could buy, racing every chance I got in front of other racing fans, hoping it would tell them that I wasn't afraid. Which in other words told me that I wasn't afraid of the boogeyman or death. It may take some time for you to see this in your life; however, you can take a close look at yourself and the people in your circle. If you look for the differences between you and me or any other persons then you're afraid to see in yourself, there you will find the differences, trust me here. If you do, you will see that this enemy was there long before now. If you really take an honest inventory of your life, you may find out when and where you began sleeping with this enemy, or what traumatized you in the first place. Now do you have an idea of what PTSD is?

I use the term "hiding place" in hope that with it I may show you some of the many faces of the enemy that we sleep with. There are many, many other terms I could have used. While you are here let's sit awhile and talk about some of these many faces a little longer and also some of my other places that I hid in. It is my hope that it may help you identify some of yours. Many of these came from my first tour of duty from the Vietnam War. Now don't think for a minute it took more than one tour, or that you must have multiple traumas for this to happen to you. I have seen men and women from many other wars who did only three months of duty in combat but have signs and behavior of this enemy. Not only that, I have seen men, women, and children affected by PTSD from just one trauma event in their lives. I've seen it take control of their lives from morning and throughout the day and night. We as a society didn't care enough about them so we did as others did before us with them. That was to just put them away from family, friends, loved ones and our society. So please look close here before you lock one of your loved ones away in a padded room or at home where there is no love from the people who say to them that we will always love you, knowing that is one of the first and foremost things they need. Oh yes, they will go by to see them on their birthday, Thanksgiving, and Christmas and call that love. Do you think that's all the love you will need or that they will need, those who sleep day in and day out with this enemy? What about the other times in their lives when they are balled up in a knot in bed, crying themselves to sleep, hiding from the boogeyman or monster that comes out at night?

Now here is a place of hiding that I took to because of some of my secrets; this one was within some of my relationships. Now let's see how this came to be one of my many hiding places; in that place I had someone who really didn't know who I was or what was going on. That relationship was about having someone who told me that I would be all right, you know, to have another person who said to me in that dark place what I needed to hear. With this I told myself that I was all right no matter what others said about me or to me. The only thing that did was help the enemy push me far away from self and closer to it. You see, I already had that secret within me, that there was a boogeyman or a monster that came out in the night. Not to say anything about my dreams. I got help with that and so can you, so stay with me here.

Relationships take on a whole new level of life if you are not true to yourself and the other person, like lying and cheating, and the things that come with them like depression, anger, and resentment. Now when we go into that world, we can lose help from the very people, places, and things that we as humans not only need in life, but also want like wives, children, and being a part of our society. From that behavior we also help some of the world and our peers see us from their old belief system or are you one of the million who live in a glass house and say to the world that you have nothing to hide or no dirty laundry to air out.

Let's talk here for a while and see what this can do to our family, starting with our mother, father, and siblings, down to wives and kids. Remember when I said that this enemy PTSD also can sleep with the family? Well, here is one of the ways it gets to stay with us during the day and the night. Got it yet or are you still looking at differences rather than the similarity, so that you might save your face, not your ass? If so the time has come to look at yourself in that mirror and see which one of them you are trying to save? Take a moment alone and see where some of your answers are coming from—is it you, or is it from this enemy living in your head rent-free? That enemy will tell you that it would be shameful to ask any family member or anyone else for a small amount help with this problem. We all know that the mind is a terrible thing to waste, so please stay with me here, if not for you then for your loved ones. So, when it comes your time to hear their cry for help, and believe me, the time will come sooner or later, we all need some kind of help if we are going to face this monster or boogeyman that we think is living in the closet or under that bed.

Other people who can come to sleep with enemy include women and children who have lived in abusive relationships, mothers who have lost children in childbirth or have seem them die right in front them, or fathers who have been in an accident with a loved one who died in their arms. All these things bring trauma and this enemy that can truly sleep with us thoughout our lifetime. Many of us don't seek help or don't know that we need help, but I'm here to tell you that if you do or think you do, help is out there just waiting for you to ask for it. Please don't be afraid to tell on this enemy that lives from within.

For a very long-time people of my generation didn't think going to a psychiatrist was cool, so not only did I live in the darkness but my information came from the dark ages. So, let me be the first of many to tell you there is no shame in seeking help for this illness, or just as sure as the many that have died with this enemy, we can become one of them if we don't let anyone in. It could happen to you also. I'm not going to sit here and talk all day about this enemy knowing that he still sleeps with me some days and knows me very well by now and I'm hoping that I won't see his new face. In hope that he want take me back so with that I won't be one of those person that will tell you that he not still out there try to take family and other by any means necessary.

There's a lot of work that still needs to be done, so let's not stop ;here; and give it power. We know that this illness will do anything to take us out. To this day it has killed a million and wants to kill many others; it is one of my beliefs now that it doesn't just want to kill you. It wants to live with you so that it may take over your family. And with that takeover it can cause more mental health, you can see what it's doing to our society today, causing us to turn on each other like animals, not humans. This has happened in so many different places, some of those places being where some of these shootings have taken place without any understanding of that person's sudden behavior. Now hear me good with these words: he is there, so don't let him do to you what he has done to others before you. Until you become one of those who will say something after something or someone has been taken from you. I am talking about one of those persons who are close to you. In ways that you didn't know, right here is where you can begin to educate yourself, friends, and family on what to come not only from trauma, but also from all the stress we live with today. That, too, is a part of this disorder, PTSD.

There are so many more parts of this enemy that we will be talking about later down the road in this book, so if you haven't got a feel for this enemy as of yet, sit back and read on. There are many other parts about this enemy, PTSD, that I will talk about, and you will see for yourself many of the events that went on in my life on this long road to recovery that I took to get out of some of my darkest places and come into light and with some of the peace that I have in my in my life today. The cost is high but I'm sure the price you pay won't be half as much as the loss of just one of your loved ones or anyone close to you, like a family member, friend, or just a neighbor who became a part of your circle. Now these are some of the ways this enemy stayed in my life for years. Let's see some other ways that I fought with the enemy long before I had the courage to ask for help and let someone into my dark world. So please don't take as long as I did or fight as hard as I did to keep my secret.

One of the worst, darkest places was with drugs. You see, this was a place I could go where people, places, and things were doing what I thought I wanted and needed to do—run from myself. This was something I could do, and my family, friends, and society looked at it and not me. You want it to be something other than what it really is, and that includes self, so take a long, hard look at the ways the enemy used its hiding place to keep me safe in my own mind. I was given drugs to help me cope and to stop the pain and the nightmares, so take it from me, being in this hiding place I was being held hostage in my own mind for years, and not talking about street drugs. Why am I talking about this? Because we need to talk about prescription drugs. They are the first thing that today's doctor wants to give people with this enemy, PTSD. However, this is something you will have to think long and hard about, I believe, because MEDICATIONS do work. Sometimes they are good. I just don't want you to stay on them for a lifetime and think that they're the only thing that will work.

I hope that you are clear with what I am trying to say here about medication. Get them from a doctor who has the right knowledge and training with PTSD. After many years sleeping with this enemy, I now know and have seen too many people get many different side effects from some of the drugs they took to help them with this enemy that added more problems. From my experience and seeing fellow veterans using medication and get other problem with the many parts of the enemy that came up in their lives, I just want you to think hard about this and get the right help. I know it's out there like counseling, psychiatry, and many other forms. And with the help of some Vietnam veterans, help has now come a long way with treatment with this enemy.

I am going to leave this chapter now because there is so much more we have to talk about other than the unknown. Hopefully from some of my unknown you may find some of your and won't have to sleep with this enemy as long as I did or have as many nightmares or flashbacks. Remember, if no one else is there for you, I am and many others who are fighting to stay alive while sleeping with this enemy. Hold on, help is on the way from many others who are living longer and help more with their information. Also more doctors now know that this enemy is real and is a threat to our society that has to be dealt with.

CHAPTER 2

The Good, Bad, and Ugly (Healing)

THERE ARE MANY ways that this enemy not only affects you but lives with you as well. For myself I found out that there is the good, which comes from some of our good experience that you will read about. Then there are the bad ones that we don't want to talk about to anyone in fear of being a bad person in their eyes, and things that we think we will need to take to our grave. Then there is the ugly—you know the ones that we think are so ugly that we block out our own memories. These are the ones that we will need a lot of help dealing with and finding some way of taking ownership of these. So what I will try to do is to open these doors so that you and others can start the healing process together.

I'll start with the ugly first, because I don't want to leave you at the end of this chapter with open wounds. So, if you are ready for this journey, let's get started. On this journey of mine I am going to tell you about my ugly that I almost took to my grave because that's where THIS ENEMY was trying to take me. This was when I thought that I was a coward; this is what happened to me in that war I talk about a lot with you. I must have been in my teens and was on a mission on Highway Four in Vietnam. One day my squad and I were controlling that highway in a personnel carrier when we came under attack from VC. Now as squad leader I was riding up top, and my men were inside of the carrier. The VC hit it with a heat-seeking missiles, meaning when it hit metal, it will first go through the metal before it explosion. With that one shot it took fifteen men out of my life; not only had they become my personal friends, but they had also saved my life many other times on the battlefield. With this one ugly thing in my life, the enemy told me for years that I was a coward and no good. However, what the enemy wanted me to believe about myself and others was untrue. Like I wasn't good enough to take care of my own family, so for years I did things to stay away from them in fear of getting them hurt. This is just one of the ugly incidents that happened to me.

Here's another one that happened to me with some of the VC children that we as soldier had to deal with for years, not only what this enemy said to us when we were alone but also what people in this country said about us when we returned home. You see, the enemy of that war knew how much we American love kids and some days they would use them to kill soldiers in great numbers. There were many days when we would see children sitting on a hill, or just standing in a rice paddy with a bomb strapped to them. Right there sometimes you had a choice to go around. Here's where another one of those ugly choices had to be made if you were to live or die, or possibly saves other lives. Now this wasn't pretty, but one of us was left behind that day. However, the enemy came to me after that incident and slept with me and my family. I guess you would ask how I knew. Well, after healing and talking to my children and hearing their stories and answering their questions about some of the ways I treated them and some of my crying in the night, I found out that that was one of my ugliest. There are many other ugly events that happened in my life for years. That's when I first found out about my kids. You see, this enemy will affect them also; there are many other parts of this ugly enemy that we carry around with us during the day from within, and most of all don't forget that we sleep with this ugly enemy too.

Now these are some of my examples of the ugly side of this enemy that I go through throughout my days,maybe you don't go through things like this in your days.s If the difference was the first thing that came to mind, maybe it's time to ask you a question. That is if you are one of us that has had some little or big ugly things happen in your lives, from some kind of trauma. Let me throw a stone in the lake here and see if you can see within the ripple effect from some of those wave. Just with any one of these uglies one in mine, from inside out, walking around with it in my home must have had everyone on pin and needles. Not knowing what to say or when to say it, fear from your father, mother, sister, or brother. Just think what it must have been like to sleep with that person or people all night, night after night. What would your childhood would have been like? The next ripple affects the person you sleep with (wife, husband, and family), if you are blessed enough to still have them in your life by now. So, with however many you have in your home or in the household you get the picture; if not, ask yourself another question. A little about the outer wave that means something from your home that affected you so hard that it hit home. For instance, your neighbor, the job, school, and church, just to name a few of them. Now your list could be short or longer than mine, but we are not looking at that. What we are looking at here if you haven't forgot is the similarity unless you still are locked in with the enemy voice or just running, not knowing where you are going.

So, you can see some parts of the ugly of this disease is the trauma itself that could send us into hiding for many years. This enemy brings mental health issues like depression, anger, and sleep deprivation, which are just the tip of the iceberg, not to say anything about all the things that happen to our mind, body and spirit. The road to recovery is no walk in the park. I am not talking about these things to put fear into you, but for you to face some of them and recover; trust me here. However, some of these questions only you can answer because the only person that knows what your truth is. These ugly things that get in our lives come from many traumas that we had in our lives; now for me some of these also were a blessing because they caused me to take a look at myself on a deeper level. There are people in our society who will do anything to save face, and that can be true for others, but me, that's not my truth anymore; so if you are one of us who lives with this enemy, then you don't have the luxury of that. What you can do is try to do this work and ask for help.

However, there many other ways I have seen this enemy known as PTSD enter and destroy lives and families, hell, whole communities.

Some of these traumas come in places where there have been hurricanes or floods where some people got swept away or taken up with no sign of them to be found. That's where some trauma can enter into whole towns and they become fearful and have flashback when they hear about another storm headed their way. Would you say that these could one of our ugly traumas when the victim was a baby or one of our children? So, you see there are many ways the ugly parts of this disease or enemy can get into our lives. Now if you want to live your life running away from self and family, you can. I would suggest that you look at what is going on in your life today. This means slow down,sit back,and listen to your heart,not your head,because this enemy lives there more than you think once he begins to sleep with you.

Now let's talk a little about the bad, and as I always do, I will tell you some of my bad, which came from war and fighting in the jungle of South Vietnam. This may be painful to some because your loved ones have been in that war or any war and may or may not have talked about these things with you. That's all right because just like the enemy, there is a place in life where healing has to begin and fear and running have to stop. So, if this healing has to start with you, hopefully it will end with them. You have to remember that some of my bad came to me because I was ordered or because it was duties. These will be some of the hardest things for me to talk about; in war some things just have to be done, not to say that it made a difference to the enemy because it didn't.

Being eighteen and ordered to go out and kill someone was traumatic all by itself. However, being in the service and a soldier and we were at war, you could say being a soldier that was my job. You see, I was drafted in the first place, told to do something that I didn't want to at all, but being a good citizen, I did what I was told. My thinking at the time was that is what good citizens did. Without knowing what was coming down the road for me or my family, I did it. If you would ask me today would I do it all over again I probably would say yes. Doing that at that time and place was a part of my freedom, I believe, in our society and not only for myself but for my seed. As you can see it also makes our country a better place for mankind. So we travel down this journey with this enemy I have come to know as PTSD. Now don't let it get you into playing the blame game, or the what-if game, for if that happens then you could be lost for many more years, and you may continue sleeping with this enemy from hell for many more years to come.

Let's see here if I can find another one of my bad, in hopes that you won't be still looking for the difference. This one had me stuck for many months before the enemy that I didn't know crept into my life. What happened was I made my first kill on the battlefield; you see, all that I ever heard from my grandmother all my life was *thou shalt not kill* and here I was killing. What I thought I was doing was killing the enemy, not knowing that I was also letting one into my life. With my first kill that person face stayed with me night and day. Until I got some courage from the people who kept saying to me, "Daddy, what's wrong? Why are you crying at nights and throughout days?" with me saying things like "I am sorry" and "Please go away." Then and only then did I stop running and start fighting this enemy back. Now I won't try to tell you it was me; that would be a lie. Many other doctors, my family, along with THE LORD JESUS CHRIST helped with some understand, as special the one who I believe is the creator of all mankind.

Hopefully you won't leave here because of my faith or my spiritual belief. There will come a time on this journey you will find your faith in something that you will call upon many a night. I believe there is only one true god, and he is the creator of all mankind. I know he helped me and stopped me from taking many other lives after I returned from that war, including my own life. If you stay with me here, I will try to help you get some of these bad faces of this enemy out of our lives so that you will know them for many years to come. You will be able to face the enemy from some of your bad side of life. This is going to take a lot of work. I know you're asking yourself a few questions, first and foremost, what else can come from the bad part of PTSD, it could be shame and guilt. With this problem there could be new worlds this enemy can take you through; I know you can relate to this. Well, for me there was a time when I wouldn't go outside for feeling or knowing any of these things. Now for shame it first came at home with my children, then it was with you. You see with that incident with the children from that war I saw their faces on your children and mine. For the fear that I thought could be seen in my face when I was with children the enemy told me that the world could see that shame on my face when I was around them and others. Now for you it may have been something that happened to you when a child was under your care, so don't think that just because you weren't in a war or something as troublesome as mine, right there if you do then you become one of those who are looking at the difference not the similarity. Without looking at the difference see if you can find some of these bad traumas that may have happened to you somewhere in your life, or look in the deepest part of your heart, soul, or spirit and you may have some of my same feelings. I just have one thing to say to you—ask yourself what part of the enemy has shown his face from some of your bad trauma. The bad side of this enemy can be something that we as humans have been running from just because of our makeup as human beings. You see, we as humans want to believe that we don't really do anything bad, that the gateway for this enemy enter in our lives. This could be a difficult part to take a good look at, but we must if we are going to defeat this enemy. Right here with these bad my hope is that we won't stay away from the truth about ourselves; if we do we won't find the whole truth about ourselves and do the work needed to be done to live a great life with oneself, family, and society.

That leaves only the good to talk about in this chapter. Now if you are anything like me, you will be asking yourself how can good trauma turn itself into something that could become an enemy out to kill or destroy me? Well, I am glad you are asking yourself that question. Here are a few of what I would say were good traumas in my life that helped me see this enemy from that point of view. Well, there was one time in my life that I guess this enemy came into my life from one of those kinds of trauma. I guess it was living deep within me waiting for something to trigger it to bring it forward. Now being a black man and living through the civil rights time, I saw people being beaten and mistreated. Some of those kinds of trauma were waiting for the right moment to show their head. When the time came for us as a people to be given freedom and not have to worry about those kinds of thing happening in our country anymore, it became a good thing. Now when I got to Vietnam and saw some children going through similar trauma, this enemy told me it was starting all over again. What happened to me then was unthinkable to myself, out of anger and in rage the enemy brought through my mind that I was right there where my family and I had been before. Now this was a different country and people from the faces of the people of my country who did this to me, so it brought out some real hate in me that helped me to hate others without thinking that the very people I was fighting were God's children also.

With this trauma coming up from within my spirit I got depressed when I saw what I did to other human beings. Like when I saw the little children crying for food that they didn't have, and I did, or when I saw some of their babies being born. It should have been a wonderful experience having two children of my own back home, but this enemy within says nothing pretty about those babies. Another trauma can be seeing someone saved from danger, and the horror of you thinking about them dying may stay with you and become a trauma, so don't look at these good traumas as something that can't and won't come back and bite you in the butt. They can and will if you are not on top of them; this enemy has ways of turning them into nightmares or flashbacks so please look at all parts of these kinds of trauma.

The good trauma can hold you hostage differently from all the rest of trauma that you may have in life. So, when I talk about the good and how it can hurt in the long run just as the ugly and the bad trauma can, believe me here by taking all traumas seriously. That means seeking help for anything that causes you to act out with some of these behavior that I have talked about in this chapter.

I know that when I found out that some of the good trauma was something I had to talk to someone about, that's when I began the fight for my life and my family's lives too. These traumas don't have to happen to everyone, but if you find any similarity in my story, then I would suggest that you seek help.

I will close this chapter with these traumas in all shapes, sizes, and forms, so don't count any of your traumas out before questioning yourself. When you begin to see some difference in the way you act from some of the little things that bring on anger, depression, shame, and guilt—from things that make tears and the heart pump a little faster, you and I know it's better to be safe than sorry. Do you want to save face or your ass? There are people who have walked a mile in your shoes, so you don't have to. Now with this information you don't have to walk on this journey alone or die with this disease known as PTSD. Come on, let's help our fellow man have a happier life for himself and his family. So please stand up, get help today, or tell a friend by giving him love from the ones who went before him. You must know with some of these traumas, some gave some and others gave all, just for you and me to live. THANK YOU.

CHAPTER 3

It's an Inside Job (Cause and Effect)

THERE ARE MANY ways that someone can sleep with this enemy that I have come to know as PTSD. So, before you start looking at whatever causes some of your effects, I would like you to do this; it will help you to have a better life. Some of my causes and effects came from a war and the things that come with wars; that is not to say that my causes are any greater or lesser than yours. I believe that you need some understanding about this first and foremost.

The point is that we all can sleep with this enemy in one way or another, which can bring with them some mental illness problem from our trauma, and see some similarity in them in many ways.

From my experience and with some healing and help from others and many of those doctors who I talk about earlier in this book,

I am taking a chance to help change our society's views and ideas about this mental health disorder with Post-Traumatic-Stress-Disorder. By now you should have a little understanding from what you have read about this enemy so far, so let's get to work and look at some of those causes.

As always, I will tell you about some of my causes, which may not be anything at all like yours. What I would like for you do is just look at some of them and see if you can find some similarity in mine in hopes that you can see if you are sleeping with this PTSD enemy. If so then you will know that there is help out there, and that you not alone on this journey, most of all that help is on the way, so you won't be sitting some place in life that you can't get out of. Because your life is waiting on you. What I don't want to do is to traumatize you any more here.

Remember that most of mine are from the Vietnam War so they can be different; however, some of the help that I got may or may not help you but by looking at some of mine, you will know that you can find help for yours, I hope, from somewhere.

The first big one I would say was from seeing someone being killed for the very first in my life at a young age, then having to kill someone at an early age in life; all of these left me with some trauma that I didn't have a clue at the time that bothered me. So sometimes you can see something that the mind cannot process properly; this could be where this enemy begins to live with us. Now we as people have a belief system that tells us that we are all right as long as we don't have to let anyone else know what is going on inside of us. Right there I let him in and from that day on I saw things that I was doing like sitting in my room for days and not sleeping at night because this enemy would bring back some of those events night after night. After that came many other things in my life like drugs and alcohol; now these are some of the last places those affected my life. Now don't look at some of these effects and run away. I just wanted you to see some of these effects so you won't have to go there. Now let's look at some of the ones this enemy used to make me think that I was a bad person, and that was why no one wanted to be around me.

One of those was isolation from my loved ones; then there was withdrawing from life itself, you know, like not going outside or doing those things that I once liked to do. You see with this enemy there are a lot of ways that it takes you away from life but it also sends you to places that only people who have slept with the enemy would understand. Others can't even when you try your best to tell them or ask them for help. By the way, this, too, is one of the effects of this enemy; it tells you that no one is going to know what you are talking about or what you are going through and that you're all alone. I am here to tell you that you're not alone and never have to be alone again. (Trust me on this.)

Now these are some of my extreme experiences; they don't have to be yours. The fact is I want you to get an idea of who and what you're dealing with here. There are some things in life that can be this extreme and lead people to sleep with this enemy; however, for others, simply seeing a dog or cat run over can lead to someone sleeping with this enemy. Now after years of seeking help and finding others who went through some of these effects, I found information about this enemy, so when others told me that it was real, I knew for sure that it was. Let me share another one that didn't seem like it was a harmful trauma, but this enemy showed up in my bedroom in the form of nightmares and in the day through flashbacks. This may not seem to be something that could cause trauma in anyone's life but for me it did. You see, when the military sent me a letter that welcomed me to the army, little did I know that that would be something that would traumatize me for the rest of my life. For me and many others this was like being raped, to have to do something that you didn't want to do, not being able to do anything, just like being made to have sex when you didn't want to. This caused a trauma to me at that time and place in life I didn't process properly. You must know that trauma can be anything that you go through and don't have the right tools to process those events. Not to say anything about after going through this event, not having the right people or doctor with the knowledge or the information about the enemy that comes into many people lives, from some of these internal wounds within the mind. So, you can see here that this isn't something that is just coming around—this is an enemy, PTSD, that has been with us for many years. It's just now that our society is getting the right information and knowledge to deal with it. This is so they won't do what others did before them. I am here to tell you that you are not alone and will never be alone again. I, along with others, am here to help you if you are sleeping with this enemy or know someone who is. We would like to make sure that you won't be locked away in one of those places of hiding. What you know from reading one of the earlier chapters is that your life and family are waiting for you to come out and give them the love that they want from you and receive the love they have for you.

Now you may have some idea where I am going to ask you to go here, and hopefully you will go with me so that you can see some of the many faces of this enemy PTSD. You may also find some cause and effects that may be keeping you from living a full life. Better yet keep others from trying to control your life or keeping you from becoming the true person that your creator intended you to be. So, are you ready to take a look at some of these traumas? They have a lot of people living in fear, and our family and society think that we are people who will hurt others or don't belong in open society. We know that people believe that they are normal, think that we are people with a disease and not an illness. By now from what you have read in this book, you should know that you don't have a disease but an illness. My prayer is that you will come out of your hiding places and reclaim your life and take back your joy.

There is something else I would like to talk about before closing this chapter. Here are some ways that this enemy that I call PTSD can get to sleep with a lot of people. Now some of these we want to take an in-depth look at so that this enemy won't run free with your thoughts or get to sleep with you another day or night.

One of those I talk about is relationships. If you got stuck somewhere with relationships, widen the picture and you can see it from your childhood through adulthood. If that doesn't work just take it where you are right now to see if there was any trauma that happened within some of those relationships. Did any one of those relationships have traumatic causes with effects that have held you back from any other relationship?

There are many other small traumas in life—some from what happened to us, others that we saw happen to others. Now this doesn't mean that they can't have the same effect or cause the same kind of behavior or mental disorder that I have or others have. We won't all act the same way with this disorder. A person could have been traumatized from see a cat getting hit by a car and still sleep with this enemy and go through the same kind of nightmares and flashbacks along with all the other things that come with this enemy. All I am asking you to do is look at some of your own cause and effect from some of your trauma. Hopefully reading this will help you know that you are not one of those people about whom our society is saying you don't have a future or a life to get back to. Don't let them hold this enemy over your head that they don't have a clue about. So, as I said before, get up out of those hiding places that we found on this journey and take back your life, not only the love you have for self, but the love you have to give to your family and world, and to receive the love that they have been waiting to share with you. With that said, here it is again, right up and personal: this enemy PTSD is not a disease but an illness.

Let's see if I can talk about one more, not because these are the only ones that may find their way into your bed or your house but, so you will know that there are many different ways we can suffer with this illness, they are mentally, emotionally, and physically. These are some of the effects of abuse or other trauma that may cut you to the bone without ever cutting you at all. It may take years of letting go of the feeling or sound from those traumas before you can go out the door from the fear of what would happen to you or see that happen to others. This is one that might come so close to us that if we think it's being played out on another, it sends us into a fear that causes us to run from life, not to it.

Then there are traumas like being caught in a bad storm where many lost their lives or in a fire or something where you were the only one to come out. Your chances of coming out were next to none, but you made it where many others didn't. Things like this can happen and do happen and leave many traumatized. Now from these traumas no one knows the answer to the cause or effect or what category to put them in. However, there is one thing we know and that is many think they can handle it. We know, just like I said sometime back, until it happens to you, we will never know the full cause or effect or what degree of trauma it will leave on us. All I know is that PTSD can and will begin sleeping with us on our journey through life if we don't get some help. No one can really say when or where this enemy begins to sleep with us. The thing is I am here to let you know that I for one slept with him, got help, found my true self, and took back my life with some peace not only for myself but for my loved ones who missed me and just wanted the real me back. Not the person that people thought they knew—people who didn't know a thing about this enemy or just knew what someone else had told them about it or what they heard on television.

So get up from there and put up a good fight, if not for yourself then for the next person who may get put away in some of those places that I talk about. Or worse, being told those same old lies that they are lost from themselves and to this society.

Love, Peace, and Happiness.

CHAPTER 4

Part 2 Cause and Effect (Family)

THERE IS ALWAYS cause and effect in life, so let's take a closer look at the causes from trauma that can bring about PTSD in our lives and in the lives of our family members and the effect it has on the people who are very close to us. We have seen some of the effects that trauma causes in other lives; however, there are many ways it affects the lives of our loved ones. We know that if we are going through some change, then it affects the world around us. To say that it doesn't would be lying to our self, first and foremost. Now let's see about our emotions, feelings, and actions. You know that in some areas of our lives there is some effect from the very beginning from whatever. Among them are depression and anger, just two that I will start with first. When we are depressed, the effects it has on our family are things like fear, separation, or walking on eggshells around us. These things will always not only keep our immediate family members away, but also keep the faraway family members at bay, so you can see that with our depression the effect can play a major role in the whole family. The fallout is that it also causes depression to others within the family. Now with that depression it won't let our family member be free to have guests over like they would like to, because of the fear of our mood swings that change from day to day. So you can see with this one effect that the cause could travel along way down the family tree. These are just some of the ways that PTSD could affect our family member. There are many other ways it could cause trouble with our family lives that we must talk about at this point. What we need to keep up front is there is help for them. After all, help can cause the opposite effect; my hope is that those who need help will seek help for depression.

Now let's take a look at anger and its effect on our family members. Some of that anger could make it harder for the younger family members; they could have a hard time getting along with their peers, not to say anything about themselves. You see, anger can come with PTSD; that is something that may have come from something we did or what we didn't do in one of our trauma situations. However, living with that anger can take on a new life with our children's and our spouses; they could act some that anger out on others from the trauma you have gone through. For my children it was anger with their peers and at school, something they took from me or home from my anger. Now for my wife it could have been her coworker. So if you are having this problem with your family, take a moment and ask yourself if this enemy has started to sleep with them.

You see, that behavior was in my life after some of the trauma from PTSD that I have been talking about all along. Cause and effect can happen from many other things in life, but for me and others who suffer with PTSD, we can trace it back to some of our events with some of our trauma. I am not suggesting that is your problem. I pray that you will just take a look at these effects with some of your loved ones. There are many other effects from the cause of this enemy in our life, so let's look at another area in our lives here for a moment.

This would be hate that we carry not only for ourselves but for many other people in our lives or mishaps that happened. Now don't get confused with this because it can become our hate that may become their hate in their lives if you want to look at it from that point of view. It became the same hate for self that they found in their own way from our hate of self. Being introduced to them by us, that could become their first hate of self; they could come to believe that something was wrong with them that made you hate yourself. Then the world becomes a mirror of you to them in life and everyone and everything becomes something to hate because of whatever they can or can't understand about your pain or hurt. There is something about hate that eats at us from the inside, just where the enemy lives. Now if you are one of those who believe that there is no truth to this, then just maybe you could take a deeper look and see if part of your behaviorare really in your children's, wife's or family's lives or are you in denial. Look into the mirror and see if the enemy of PTSD has taken over or if you are just hurting too bad to ask yourself this hard question. This could be the time and place where you can get some help for yourself, or maybe for your loved ones. Take this time, and to thy own self be true. There is one thing about hate: wherever it lives there is always anger, something that we already talked about. Now there is resentment that we can see as an other parts of this enemy. All these faces or parts of PTSD can be helped with the right people, so let's not stop here but move on into the future of life with a new look at this illness disease that many now known as a mental illness.

We have looked at some of the effects trauma has on our family and in our home. Now let's look at some of the effects that it can have on our society. Our community sees us with a mental health problem, people who need to be put away from the world so that we won't be with others, or around our family and friends. You could say that our society think the worst about people with this mental health issue. They have the right to think the way they want to, but we don't need to be locked away in some mental home. What we do need is proper medical care with the right people who know, first and foremost, what PTSD is and how it affects people. Its effect on our society could come from being misinformation about PTSD. This leaves a big question for our society to ask. Is there Post-Traumatic-Stress-Disorder in our time, then what about our past veterans and other who had been traunatized in the past.

There is another cause and effect that I would like to talk about here before we leave this chapter. This one has to do with children who come from a traumatized family. I am talking about the problem that our society says that it's all right for our children to play war games or any other game that leaves some of them with trauma. I know you don't think of it as a trauma, but it's a trauma to the mind that may make a hole for the real feeling. Look at what is going on with our sons and daughters who have problems with authority figures. Maybe you don't want to look at this because your children don't have a problem yet and I do say yet because as we know anything is possible. If not that then look at the bullying going on in our school system. Also what is going on in the mental health field with children who either play these games or are around others who play them. You can see some of the cause and effect that happens to others, not just to those of us who have been in a war or are around people who were in wars. Now from here on this journey of learning you will see this enemy and I do say enemy because you see the thing with PTSD is that it affects many other areas in our lives. So please don't let this chapter go to waste, for reasons that you don't understand or don't have a lot of information about it. I am not a doctor or a physician; these are the best people to go to for this information. However, being a person who has lived with this problem for over thirty years, there is something that I can share from my experience while living with this enemy. So I pray from the bottom of my heart that you get help with this, if not only for yourself, but for the many people it may affect in your life or your circle. If you would bring that circle in closer then you see that we will be talking about our wives, children, and self. Don't be one of those people who will just sit there and tell themselves there is nothing wrong. After all you have heard and read what I have said in this book, then ask you self why did it call out to you?

What I would like you to do as I get ready to leave cause and effect is for you to look at just one day in your life from this day on. Let me be the first one to tell you that we won't leave anyone behind. It's your time to come out and live your life and have a life with your family and friends.

Me Do Love You

CHAPTER 5

Wounded (Internal)

THERE ARE MANY wounds that veterans of wars and others suffer from, but when you talk about them, most people can only see the external wounds. However, there people who have internally wound who need help also. Many other veterans of wars and I have internal wounds, and what we suffer with, is known as PTSD, which has caused many veterans and their family to live in hell. Now from my thirty years of living with this enemy and the internal wounds, I would like to take you on a journey with some of what I have experienced with this illness on a personal level and what my family along with our society have gone through. One of the first things I will talk about is from the last chapter with cause and effect living with this enemy; that's right, this is an enemy that we not only sleep with but also have to live with daily. You see, this enemy tells you from the inside where the wound is that you wounded and don't have an illness. With that in mind let's see if I can open your eyes to a little reality about it.

From the very beginning of talking about this enemy, I would like you to know that the medical field sees it as a mental problem. From that view it took over my life and others who didn't have any knowledge of PTSD, not knowing too much about these internal wound, only looking at external wounds, and not knowing the importance of having the right knowledge of this wound in veterans and others who suffer with this enemy. What I know and have experienced is what started at home, then moved throughout my circle in life.

You see, these wounds are so personal that they told me I was all right and to keep it to myself. That's when it became the enemy from hell that not only did I sleep with, but I haved to live with for the rest of my life. At first, I looked at it like something I didn't want my family to know anything about, and then it became something that I didn't want anyone to know either. There were many reasons for this; here are a few that I will tell you about so that you can get an idea just how this enemy PTSD survived in our family.

My problem began when I was trying to get a job and wrote on the application that I was diagnosed with PTSD, and that being a mental health condition, my application went to the bottom of the job listing. You might ask why is that? Well, what I was told once is that rules for that condition were too much of a risk. Now being someone with an external wound that could be seen, and nothing could be said about those from the misinformation that had been given to our society about internal wounds and the condition of a person's state of mind. You see, not only for us is the right information something we need to know, but it is something our society needs to learn about also so that when their employees need it, so that people with this mental illness want their job and will be able to find good jobs. This was my first experience with my internal wounds and how the world views people like myself. So now when you learn about this from those who have lived with this enemy or doctor, the right information can and will be given to the right people who have these jobs so that you and them can begin to trust yourself and others with a mental problem and show others that we can be trusted. When this society puts labels on people, it can follow them throughout their life. This won't seem very difficult for people who have not been labeled; however, for those of us nowadays with internal wounds, we must learn the truth not only for ourselves but also for the world at large.

So as you can see from my early chapter, these cause and effects just keep getting in our lives no matter who we are or where we go. This I know not from someone telling me but from living in this world with my wounds for a long time. My prayer is that you will take this seriously and take a close look at yourself so that you won't run and hide in a dark room or someplace that this enemy that we sleep with can keep you there for years without the proper help and care. Hope is something that I don't want you to lose sight of because without it you could become one of those that I talk about in the book I wrote, *MIA: Missing in America (Our Sons)*. Remember this if nothing else on this journey that we are taking, it's not only to save our lives but also to save the lives of those still to come. Remember the saying "Some gave some and others gave all." That is truth in life also, so do you see how this works with internal wounds?

When I was hit with a piece of shrapnel, the wounds weren't viewable from the outside and I received a Purple Heart for that. However, still to this day on rainy days or cold days it hurts and still have to take something for it. Now from my PTSD wounds this is also some internal pain; it doesn't have to rain or be cold for me to have emotional pain, sometimes more pain than any that come from the external wounds. These wounds bring with them more pain and suffering, not only to me, but also to my family and friends, than anyone could ever imagine. Just maybe when the time comes for you to talk about these wounds to someone, this enemy may show up in your mind and heart and try to keep your mouth from opening, no matter how hard you may want to. So here is the time and place on this journey in our life that we are a team and fellow soldiers of any war or just trauma victims. Together, no matter now different we are, or our family may seem, we can become one on this journey of healing and helping others. That will leave a light that shines so bright, it will say to this country and the world this society that sleeps with this enemy will not leave anyone behind. If nothing else comes from these wounds in my life or yours, I believe that we will help our fellow man; my belief is that what we as human beings were created for from the beginning. One of the greatest gifts that man was put on this earth for is to go through things and come out the other side to help this world and mankind to live better. When I was first diagnosed with this enemy PTSD, I thought it was the worst thing that could happen to anyone. Now don't get me wrong here, on some days I still feel that way when the enemy won't let me see the greater good in life, so always remember that "some gave some and other gave all." Somewhere in my mind I know that the men who didn't make it through on this journey didn't gave their all for nothing. You see, when you are sitting there not knowing what to do or if you really want to get help, think again—there is someone out there depending on you to make it through your journey so that they just might have a chance in life. So sit back for a moment and let your mind run free about this enemy that many of us sleep with and tell yourself, *This time I won't run from you.* What I will do this time is learn about this enemy so that it won't take another life from me or my family or any other family in my lifetime. So you see we must do our duty once again and take a stand if not for ourselves, for the many who sleep with this enemy that causes effects not only with our family but with many others we will come in contact with. Just ask yourself what many have asked before: Are we men and women or mice? Let's not leave this chapter without going that extra mile for ourselves and our loved ones who look to us for their future. I won't lie to you; this is not a journey that all will choose to take, but if you are anything like me, then the time has come where it has become a life or death choice, and I mean that from the bottom of my heart. This is not the way to look at these internal wounds, but they are helpful enough for you to start asking yourself some questions. I guess you might want to ask me what my purpose on this earth is after living with this enemy. I would say to fight for my life and others and not fall a victim to this enemy that is now trying to take our children along with our society at large. In hope that I have been used and given many the courage to share this life-giving message with you and others in my lifetime.

If you have come through some of your nightmares, flashbacks, and things that we have talked about up to this point on this journey, then just like I have said in my other books, many are called but few will stand—so welcome on this journey of learning and teaching to those who will come look for some answers. We as Vietnam veterans lost many before they got it right, and was told that it wasn't shellshock or anything else that was killing or taking so many family members hostage, but the enemy that they sleep with now known as PTSD. So thanks you for holding on this long; now we can say to that family, wives, husbands, and children that they didn't go through what they went through for nothing. We love all of you for your journey and your help with this book of life, about this enemy that still has so many faces, so many masks, and may help me keep many of us out of those dark hiding places in life. I hope you have some understanding of where to go from here, so with these places being seen with your own eyes and heard with your own ears, we must continue on this journey. I pray that you stay with me a little while longer.

CHAPTER 6

Nowhere to Run

THERE ARE A few places we talked about that you could hide, but running is something different altogether. You see, this enemy tells you that there is nothing wrong with you. First, you need to know some of the places that you may run to in life. For me there were these places that my thinking told me was where I needed to be, but the truth is they weren't. I just want you to look at this place where I hid for years. What was wrong with them was that they not only took me places I didn't want to go but took my family to places in their lives that they shouldn't had to go. You know some of them by now because I have been talking about them for a while with you. I will name a few just to see if they will get you to think about yours; or did you have some like mine or are they some of yours?

First and foremost, there was the need for adrenaline, and then there were others like relationships, gambling, and one of my longest, drugs and alcohol. These are a few that I will talk about that took me places and put my family in harm's way as well. Now if you keep an open mind here you just may see yourself in one of my hiding places. Let me talk about one of my hiding place with adrenaline; first it told me that I wasn't afraid of anything, knowing deep down inside I was afraid of myself. I didn't know anything was wrong from my internal wounds. It didn't show itself until I was alone or at night when I was sleeping within nightmares that were so frightening that I was afraid of everyone and everything. I didn't know that this enemy called PTSD worked on the mind with the use of fear. It gave me a reason to run and hide by being an adrenaline junkie, and with that it took me from racing cars to fighting and doing things that I thought showed our society that I was bad; also, it told me that whatever happened, it didn't traumatize me. Just lies from this enemy that showed up in all those places I ran to, so that I couldn't tell you or ask for help from anyone. Now this may not look like a hiding place that I talked about before, but you're going to have to trust me here—being an adrenaline junkie, you could become another addict. This was a part of this enemy that I didn't have a clue about. Now this is something that this enemy love to put in your way. You see, when I was jacked up from my adrenaline feeling, it felt like a high or courage to face anything, but the feeling always came down, and then what happened was depression. With depression there are all kinds of feelings that sent me running for the next thing to get the adrenaline juices flowing again. Which started with something I had to do that took me back time after time to this hiding place. So you see this can be a hiding place for those of us who live with this enemy which came from the trauma that we had from something. We said over and over to ourselves that it didn't bother us, but I know that at night this monster comes in our dreams or in nightmares from these traumas. There are many other things that come from being adrenaline junkie that comes from running from this enemy PTSD. So take a long, hard look at yourself and see if you see a part of me in you; then you may be able to say to yourself, "No more will I let this enemy send me into hiding. Not from myself or from the people who love me the most and need me in their lives."

With that said, let's look at another one of my hiding places that stayed with me for many years: relationships. That's right, they can become hiding places for many of us, so don't look at this hiding with the least amount of concern. Knowing most people look at relationships as a place to go for one reason or another, some of us choose to use them as hiding places, and with this one I will tell you how I used it for hiding and how it cost me my family and brought many other problems in my life. You see, if you suffer with PTSD and sleep with this enemy, it will tell you that you need someone in your life so that you won't have to be around those who will see you as you do after you come to know this enemy—also so that they won't keep asking you the same questions, "What's wrong, honey?" or "What's wrong, Father?" These people are the ones who stay with us at first, long before the enemy gets into their lives. Now after this enemy begins to sleep with our family, it reacts in everyone lives differently. In just the little time that you have seen some of the causes and effects this enemy had with my family members, the problem is if it's within you now, you need to say the right things to yourself now about it. With your truth, not mine or anyone else's, answer this question for yourself. Then you will know the answer to the statement "to thy own self be true." This is one way that this enemy can affect our family, by telling us not to be true to our self. What do you think it told them?

Here's another hiding place that you may run to. What I did was get in and out of relationships so that the person in the new one wouldn't know anything about my condition. This way I could hide in my own madness, just me and the enemy that I sleep with many nights. What that did was start a new family, giving the enemy more people to affect in my life. So you see by me not seeing these as hiding places, I caused a lot of hurt to a lot of people in my family and the families of others.

Then there are the lies in a relationship that you have with your doctor and psychiatrist. These are ways in our relationship that we hide with lies that we tell ourselves from our internal wounds that bring about this enemy that runs wild in our lives. There are many other ways to use relationships to hide and help us run from the truth. Now, you can take these hiding places with a grain of salt or let them stay in your life until they take over your life like myself and many others did and pay the price, which we all know could become death. You leave others in more pain, now they may have to have live with this enemy alone from maybe the trauma of losing you. You know from what you have read within these pages and heard on the news that we are losing this battle with the enemy called PTSD. These are just a few of the hiding places in relationships that I have found to be truly places that I found myself trying to find my way out after I confronted this enemy from within. So do you want to get a head start on this enemy or do you want to go through what I and many other, of years of suffering that we have already gone through so you won't have to? This relationship hiding place may be a place where people who suffer with PTSD hide, a place that many run to when they don't want to face life on its own terms. However, you and I know sooner or later you are going to have to face whatever you are running from. Some of the problems that come from these internal wounds with their hiding places are guilt and shame, but hiding in a relationship other than the one we started with. Possible could had been the main one that we needed to recieve some healing and grown from on this journey through life. We're always was on the run again, looking for more and different hiding places.

Let's look at another hiding place here, which was a battlefield of life and death for many years. This one is drugs and alcohol. You see, these two stopped the pain for me for many years. If I said that they didn't, I would be lying; however, I also need to tell you the truth about these hiding places: what this enemy did and what it stole from me and my family for years. Now by this being a hiding place they all were a part of the enemy that came come from internal wounds—wounds that cannot be seen but are felt from within; they will take away the only people who are really in your corner. In my time, I used street drugs. Nowadays there are street drugs but there is also medication that you can get from your doctor—both can be used as hiding places. With these two together you become known as a dual diagnosis. You see, when you have a mental problem and drug or alcohol problem, they can take you in hiding places with the two at the same time, so be very careful here when you start running from either one, knowing what this enemy would want you to do. That way it will make it that more harder for doctors to detect, also sometimes impossible to separate. So if these hiding places become comfortable, then you will know that those internal wounds are using them to keep people away, and you should know by now when we are alone in our head, we are in trouble. So from some internal wounds they came create problems for you and for your whole family. However, just because I help you to look at a few of these hiding places from our wounds point view, it's not to say that you will be one of us who runs to these places. It's just that I want you to look at some of the ones that have taken other to their grace, or have many other lost to us and theirselves. You see, this is a serious matter; that is why I needed to share my journey about my internal wounds, so that others won't think that they are living with this enemy alone and that no one is working on their behalf.

In the beginning of this chapter, I call one of these hiding places gambling, and that is true; now let me take you down this road of gambling and why I call it a hiding place. In this hiding place, you are gambling with your life. Now I know that you think it would be impossible for that to happen, so let me take you on the journey with this hiding place and now it can become a death sentence. When we gamble we are not letting anyone know what we are going through like depression, anger, fear, loneliness, separations, and these are just a few of the emotions that one feels on this journey when they are gambling with their lives. You see, when I was gambling with my life I had no idea that all the other things that I talk about in this book were a part of that gambling hiding place. Now you can be like me and lie to yourselves for years and stay alone and live in fear, or you don't have to go on these journey to these hiding place before it starts by stopping here and now and taking a look at yourself. See if this is true or a lie that I tell you about myself. Take a moment here to see if you're gambling and hiding with the lies that you tell yourself as you are reading these words. If so then come out of hiding and call the help line today because I will be there, not in person but in spirit. This hiding place can be the most dangerous of them all because when you are there, you are not only in denial, but you also give the enemy of this disease room to grow from within and these internal wound to run wild from you to all others who come in your life or are in your life today. Remember the saying that I hold true to the deepest part of my heart: We won't leave anyone behind. You see, we are soldiers in this war together; you may be one of us who has not fought in a real war, and that makes no difference because with this enemy from some internal wound we all become soldiers in war against the human race. Please, if you think that you sleep with this enemy, get help or at least find out what is going on with you and these feelings and anxiety attacks. This enemy's main objective is to tell you that nothing's wrong with you and that you could handle this if everyone would just let you be. So before you leave this chapter, think about all the people who died just to make sure that you don't have to.

CHAPTER 7

The Battle from Within

WITH THIS ENEMY there will be many battles to come. The greatest, I think, will be the one from within. That is not to say that there won't be other battlefields, because there will be; however, for now I want us to take a look at the ones you need to be aware of. You see, when you sleep with the enemy morning, noon, and night, there are many battles that will jump on you. These are ones that I say that our society won't let us live with or without. We talk about many of these in the previous chapter, so let's get down and dirty here with the other battle that we will need to be aware of if we are going to put up a good fight against the enemy that has taken so many lives and loved ones away from so many.

First, we need to know that this enemy comes from the kind of wounds that most of us have, and those are wounds that cannot be seen from the outside or with the eyes. The battle will be your head telling you that there is nothing wrong with you. Next it will tell you that you don't need help, just keep on living your life the way you are living. Some of the ways you have read about already; others you will find along the way on this journey, together and as we fighting for our lives. You see, when there is a battle going on from within, most of the time this enemy wants you to think that you alone; then it wants you to think that there is no help. I'm going to blow both of these out of the water by telling you and showing you that it's a lie and a theft that come to rob you of your life and take over your mind. However, it won't get away with it today or any other day because I'm here with the good news that this battle from within will be won by you and many others who arm themselves with the right information about this enemy, by knowing that it is alive and real. With the right help from the right people, you can and will defeat this battle from within if you believe that there are ongoing within these wounds that can't be seen from the outside but are there from many traumas that you have seen or gone through. Walk with me here for a little while longer and listen to me a little longer so that we won't let anyone else or ourselves die from not knowing about this enemy from within that many say doesn't live within our minds and thoughts.

This is a battle that we must fight to help show others who think that living with this enemy PTSD is something that they can' overcome from, and would have other believe that there isn't an enemy known as PTSD. Well, after sleeping with this enemy for some thirty years now, I'm here to tell them that this is a lie. I am here to help you and let you know that it is PTSD and there is help for you and others if you are willing to do just one thing—put down the bat and stop beating yourself up. There are many of us out here and we won't leave anyone behind, so come in out of the battlefields of fear, hate, and anger. We are here just waiting for you to come to the land of the brave and the few who still believe that you are worth fighting and dying for. There are many things worth fighting for in this world, and I believe life is the most precious of all. There are many who put stuff and things at the top of that list, but I do not.

Now, there are many ways that this battle from within comes at us. Some of them for me were through touch, smell, and sound. These don't have to be yours, but I do ask that you look for yours; they are there. These are some of the ways that this battle from within gets its beginning. However, these are not the only ways that it will attack you, so be mindful here with who and what you are doing as always. PTSD with its trauma affects everyone differently from time to time. So when things begin to go wrong and when you're in a place in life that sends you mixed feelings from within, with symptoms like crying, anger, or fear, these are some of the things that come from within where the enemy and battle first starts. There is no time or place where we can put our hand on when these things begin to happen to us; however, we all know that they do. Most of my trauma came in a war, so I had trouble with things like the scent of blood, or when a car back-fired, just to name a few. For some others who have not been in a war it could be whatever they encounter within that trauma at the time and space. There was this one man who was traumatized when he saw his wife giving birth to their child, and he was unable to have sex with her anymore. This seems harmless, but he had nightmares about that event. Somewhere along the way he found someone to help him understand what was happening to him with this enemy PTSD, most likely one of us and it came too many years later in his life. With that cause and effect, he lost his family. However, after he found out about this enemy and got help with that battle from within, I can say today at least they are friends and a family when for years they were not. Now just because you can't see the battlefield, that does not mean there isn't a battle going on; just because you can't see these wounds, that is not to say that you not wounded. So please hear me loud and clear: there is a battle going on from within, and you are not alone. Don't put off today by not asking or looking for help because there is help. If there isn't anyone but me then you know there is help. At the same time, I need you also to help me stay on top of this enemy or he will take me out like he did so many others who forgot that this battle can be a lifetime if we won't get help. So please, if you are going through this nightmare, crying or running away from what you think is a monster in the closet, he is there—PTSD. Within the mind are wounds that you may have gotten from trauma,that you throught was nothing but became something that you didn't want anyone or the world to know about. I know because I lived with him for many years and ran far too long and hurt my family along with myself. So now is the time for you to do something about it for yourself and your family; pick up the phone or better yet tell someone so you won't be the next person lost to this illness known as PTSD.

Many have said that this is something that will go away in

time, and that may be true for some; however, that wasn't the truth for me. That is not to say that you are like me or many of my friends who have lived with this enemy for thirty or more years. What makes this enemy so dangerous is that with one person it may be a few weeks and for another, years—some trauma from wars has lasted for a century. If you don't think so, look at some of the descendants from the Civil War. I have learned that when we sleep with this enemy, so does our family. Many of those traumas can last for years,and also from that same war I have seen it last only for a few years. Which are you? Do you know or can anyone else tell you the right answer to this question? What I do know is that it took many lives of other people, and some doctors told them that it was nothing, "You have to move on with your lives."

Now don't get confused with what I am saying; don't kill the messenger here. What I am trying to say is that if you think you are having some of these battles from within yourself, then don't let people with misinformation make your discussion for you. Do some research for yourself, and seek doctors who have worked with trauma victims. It starts with you and ends with you. This is your journey and you and only you know when this enemy talks to you. We are living in a time when we are responsible for our own health and welfare. So if we are going to have a fighting chance against this enemy from within, then we will have to arm ourselves with all the information that we can find from people who not only have been there but done that. Also seek out people who know this enemy from the ground up; they are out there. All you have to do is ask and they will come running, because as I said before, we won't leave anyone behind in this war against mankind. You see, when you have something like this enemy that has been around as long as PTSD has been, then we have to start believing that there is something out there that can take out a whole family. We know that this enemy attack the mind with our throughts that make you believe there is nothing wrong with you. Then just look what it has done to many of those who not only sleep with this enemy day in and day out, but are told what to believe or what not to believe. Now just look at what it has done to our professional society for years who still today don't believe that this enemy begins with some of our unseen wounds, from trauma that many of us have to fight with on a daily basis. If you live with this enemy or feel that your son, spouse, family members, or friend might be sleeping with the enemy from some trauma that you know they have been through but are not getting help with, please after you have found some help, try to help them find their way to the people or place where there is help. Just don't stand there and help them to an early grace; if you are reading this book or found a self-help program, then you already know others who need some help, so help, please. As I have been writing about in some of my other work, we as a society cannot afford to lose anyone on this journey in life. Not because I said it but because we know that any lost dream could be the one that saves this world from itself. If you are looking for something to tell yourself about this battle from within that many are fighting with every day, stop right there and listen to yourself. You will learn if you are one of the people who sleeps with this enemy. Most of all, you are in a battle from within for your life, so don't just sit there—get up and call someone or, better yet, tell that person who had your back all this time. We all have someone who has seen us at our lowest and in our worst moment with this enemy, so go ahead. He or she is just waiting for you to ask them to help you find help for yourself. Now with that said, we love you and want the best for you on this journey. However, we also need you in our lives to tell your story to those who will be going through what you went through, because we know that when we come through something, it's not just for us—it's for the greater good of mankind. So get up from there and help make this a better world from going through what you went through with this enemy and still being alive, knowing that was not his plan from the moment he told you there wasn't anything wrong with you and to keep it to yourself.

I will leave you here with these thoughts: If a man comes through something in his life, it's not just for him, but a gift from the creator of all mankind to help him and others on this journey home.

CHAPTER 8

You Are Not Alone (Help)

ON THIS JOURNEY with this enemy there are many things you will have to go through; however, you won't have to go through them alone.

When I found out that I slept with this enemy, the first and foremost thing that came to mind was that I was alone. Then came no one needs to know about this enemy but me. That was the wrong thing for me to think or believe, then I starting to live with that belief. Not knowing this enemy that well, now I know that what it needed me to believe that way it could get me on the run. So with that belief I know today that I ran from everyone and everything. With that running I ran right into the enemy's hands. That's right, not saying anything to anyone was my first mistake. However, I'm here not only to see that you don't make the same mistake that I did but also to let you know that we are out here waiting and willing to help you on your journey. You see, there are many others who live with this enemy day in and day out, but there will be some chances and risks you will have to take on this journey if you are going to be someone that survives sleeping with the enemy, while becoming someone who will help others on this journey afterward. With some of this information's you will find out that you are not the only one and will never be alone if you are willing to take some steps and do some work on your own and work with others who have survived PTSD.

There will be people from all walks of life who will be willing to help you. This is what I mean by doing some work on your own, because everyone, including doctors, therapists, and others who say they know this enemy is only giving you information from what they heard or read. Most people have not lived with this enemy or worked with anyone who has. Some people who have lived with this enemy won't have the same symptoms that you or I have, but they will understand it when they see it, when it shown up in other's lives. That's why I am telling you that you will never be alone again if you are willing to be open-minded here and do the work that I am talking about. Why? Because I'm here along with many others who are still living today after years of sleeping with this enemy, who have lost much along the way. Now let's see if we can get to a place where you feel comfortable enough to seek some of this help. I had to come to my own understanding from within where this enemy lived to find something that meant more to me than anything or anyone, before I finally got the courage to tell myself that there was something wrong here. That meant that

I got sick and tired of being sick and tired and crying, fighting with myself and everyone who was close to me. This you will find in those places where you first cry out to whatever I did, now I know it was the GOD of my understanding, who is that for you. I say that because we all call on something or someone when we are hurting bad enough from this pain that comes from within, knowing that you cannot use any of those things or places I talked to you about in the previous chapter. You may know this for yourself by now and people may have told you this long before now, but if you are anything like me, you have been there many times before, not having the courage or the strength take that step. Now you will because we here and something told you to pick up this book. Yes, we are here in spirit and in body, just waiting for others who sleep with this enemy to come forward. I know you are asking yourself, "By now do I know that or better yet why did I say that?" Because if you haven't read anything else that I wrote, I suggest that you read *Looking at You, Finding Myself.* I know it will help you with that.

Now being a veteran, the VA hospital was where I first found that person who knew something about this enemy first. If you are not a veteran, there are doctors and psychiatrists who I believe and have learned that this enemy is alive, but also remember that it is still outing to take lives, not give life. That's not to say that no one else has any knowledge about this enemy, if I would tell you that it would be a lie. These days we have lots different of ways to get information about anything we want to. That's what makes this enemy like a two-headed sword. One of the better ways for us to get help is to go to support groups where we will find people who have lived with this enemy and can share their own experience, strength, and hope. There is nothing like hearing someone tell their story, which somehow helps others get the courage and strength to tell theirs. When I heard other people talk about this enemy and the trials that they went through and were still going through, that gave me hope that I could get through it too. Now getting out there to find these groups will take some work on your part, but this is work you will have to do. However, even with that work you won't be alone because I am here and there will be many others on this journey to help you along the way. Like I was saying today with all the technical knowledge that we have, with a little work you will and can find us, so don't just sit there and let this enemy take from you what it took from me and many others. With what I know now and was told by many others who helped, I won't let anything happen to you on my watch. So you see this is a responsibility not just to us also to you too. Now get up and get out of those hiding places and find us because I need you and so do many others who need to hear your story. Maybe no one else has shared your story before, and your story could be the one that brings many out of their darkness. You see, we all are a part of this journey with this enemy, and if one person is left out then many more may die.

There is also help for our family members. I have talked about how this enemy lives within us but also it lives within our family, so don't let your loved ones down here. Once we find some help for ourselves, it becomes our responsibility to help them. Not only because we love them but because we have to protect our seed on this journey for years to come—which can mean long after we are dead and gone. Now that we have found help for ourselves from others, those same people can and will help our loved ones. Knowing what I know, I am able to look back over my life and see the many ways that this enemy took over my sons and daughter, not to say anything now, after becoming a great-grandfather and that's about my seed, so you can see how long this enemy can stay in your family and others who may have slept with you on this journey so far. You have to know that this enemy can and will move down the line from generation to generation if we don't get help and stop it before it stops us. That's why I'm pleading with you, so that your seed won't have to live with this enemy as long as mine did.

These are just a few ways that you can get help with this enemy. So don't let these few ways stop you from looking for others ways to get help, I'm here to tell you that this enemy hasn't grown with many more faces and symptoms since we as a society have started to take a closer look at it. Don't let your dreams and hopes die from not knowing what this enemy can and will do to you and other who won't go out and get help first for themselves, then for their loved ones.

You and I know from our sleepless nights and long days that the enemy lives from within us from some of the trauma, so don't let other tell to get over it you should just let it go. We know that the human mind and body have many different models, just as many as there are people and personalities in our society. So, please come with me on this journey of recovering not only our lives but our children, family, and the many who still live in some of those dark hiding places in life. This enemy has to be stopped before any other wives, husbands, or children lose their loved ones forever. Or be put away in a medical institutions for a lifetime or where there is no love or light of hope. Are you with me? If not then I'm on my way back for you because like I said, we leave no one behind. So please don't just sit there waiting on your life; go out there and take it back. Welcome home.

CHAPTER 9

The Taker of Life (PTSD)

SOMETIMES WHEN I think about where I came from and where I am today, it puts a knot in my gut. You see, it's not easy to talk about this enemy that has taken many years of my life, leaving me without a feeling of love for myself or many of my family members. Not to say anything about the time that I wasn't thankful to the god of my understanding. Also, without thinking about the many that I lost along the way. However, this is still helping me with some of my healing today. I believe that by writing this book and trying my best to help others on this journey with their healing, help me with my knowing that others in my past didn't pass away for nothing, writing has become a purpose in life for me. That's why I want you to know all that I can tell you about this enemy that is the taker of life, in hope that it won't take anymore lives in my lifetime. Knowing that with our healing you too can say in a louder voice, thank with gratitude to our creator of life. I hope that it will also become one of your purposes in life after becoming a survivor of this enemy known as PTSD. So let me get to work here and see if I can help you out of one those hiding places that we talked about so far, bring some light along with the help that you may be looking for. As you know I won't leave you or anyone else behind if I can help it. I'm not saying this just to say I have all the answers, but to let you know that when we help others, it helps us with our healing on this journey.

I know talking to others about something that is taking life not giving life can be very troublesome to some people,and the first time I heard about this enemy, the taker of life, I was afraid too. So let me see if I can help you receive this with a little bit of sugar instead of salt, some of the things we talked about awhile back. when you talk to people about the taker of life, the first thing they will think about is dying. This may be sad to hear but it can and will happen to many other that why I'm here with my story. Unfortunately, that has happened too many times, and that's why I'm here for you with a lot of others who have been through this, so that you or anyone else won't lose their life to this enemy or any of their loved ones' lives. That is not to say that we don't die—we can and will if we don't help each other with some of the work that needs to be done with them and ourselves.

One of the first things I would like to talk about here is a part of life that the enemy will begin to take from us first, and that is our spirit. When a person has a spiritual death, he/she can lose faith in themselves and others, not to say anything about losing faith in the help that comes from our spiritual father. I know that this can be a very difficult subject to talk about, being that we all have our own personal idea about our own spirituality. Now let's not get stuck here and let this enemy make us run away from each other by looking at the different kinds of religions. That's not what we are looking for here; we are looking for and talking about our spirit. You know that we all have a spirit, so when this enemy gets hold of the mind, that was when I first started to lose faith in myself and tell myself I wasn't any good or that I was worthless. That's when I stopped caring about myself and others. Hopefully here is where you can see this enemy; most of you may see where it can begin to take our life away, not only yours but your loved ones as well. This should have been the first sign of me dying from within; with that part of me beginning to to die I gave the enemy (PTSD), the key to many other parts of life for it to kill, so don't let this happen to you. However, if this is happening to you as you read these words, you will begin to feel it from within yourself where your thinking takes you as these words enter your spirit from these pages.

There are many things about dying a spiritual death that happened to me that I didn't see for many years. The other was my emotion that I talk a little about a few chapters back. When I wrote *Looking at You, Finding Myself (Oneness)* I talk about us all being a part of everything and everyone on this journey in life. By knowing that, I got a better feel for how this enemy can and will take life and destroy our family from within. So don't let it convince you here that you can handle this all by yourself when you don't have to. In the same breath you will feel from within what I mean when I say to you that this is a life-taking enemy called PTSD. Now hold onto this and don't let that part of your life die anymore or better yet don't let this enemy start its death- run. (The spirit of a man is what keeps him alive; his experience in life is what helps him to stay alive.)

Now let's look at another one of the ways this enemy takes lives from us and our loved ones: our emotions. That's right, it kills our emotions, and if we are not on top of this killer, it will take us out. You see, when something kills a person's emotions, it limits his ability to feel good or bad, right or wrong. When these things first start to take place in my lives, I begun to die in many ways, most of them unnoticeable. First of all I stop loving myself first, then others. I know now that it affected my emotions so bad that I had no feeling about things that were happening to me or others—like when I did something that should have made me show some kind of emotion like sadness, happiness, or gratitude for what I had accomplished or didn't accomplish, there was no emotional feeling at all. This enemy (PTSD) being to kill my emotions from within, pushing me close to death, helping me to believe those lies that no one cared or I was worthless—along with anything that made me feel less, then it gave me thoughts of hurting myself. With thoughts like that we all know what can come to mind next. These kinds of thoughts run through our mind on a daily basis, so that this enemy has to be stopped here and now. Some of these things that I will be talking about in this chapter may not be the same kinds of things that you're going through with the enemy, but this enemy is alive and will try to take life, not give it. Look for the similarities in my experience; once you begin to look at the differences in my story or anyone else's, you become this enemy PTSD's subject and we all know where that can lead.

When we lose some of our emotions , there are a lot other things in life become unwanted, like love, caring, and hope for any kind of future. So you can see here if you are one of us who have died to any of these things, then I'm on my way back to the scene of the crime to help you out of that foxhole in life. Now some of these places that we run to when this enemy starts to take life from us are not pretty. By sharing some of these experiences I pray that I can help others with some of the knowledge I gained along the way and how I fought for my future and children's future. So be careful here because we know what happened to others who said that they didn't need any help with this enemy, lose not only themselves but their family and children along the way. Just look what happened to some of our ancestors who got caught up in the racial war and the civil rights time. To this day they still have some of their seed lost to this society, who didn't know or want any help with this enemy PTSD. So you see from this enemy many have been taken from their loved ones, and it may have been the one in your family or my family who could have helped save this world in one way or the other. When I look back over the years that I was walking around dead inside without any kind of emotion, I was not sharing with my loved ones my love or able to receive any of the love they tried to give me. I didn't talk about any of my emotions that I could have shared with others as I passed through their lives. So it seemed they were afraid of me but they weren't; they didn't know what I would do to them or others without me being able to show some emotion of feeling. Without showing some kind of love or caring for me or others, you could say that my family, friends, and our society had to think only what others had said about me was true. So go on, take your lives back from this enemy here and now by letting yourself know that it's okay to need help and make sure that this enemy won't win. With that smile and hope, with some love for yourself, your future will look brighter, as well as your family's future. Now just for a moment sit there and feel the life come back into your body, so you will know that this enemy is coming down and coming down hard.

There are many things that will come out of this chapter that will help you to know if you need help or if you are going to run from this enemy. You are dying from within from this enemy that is killing you and others slowly. We all know that we all have to die one day but let's not die from this enemy now that we have new information about it. When this enemy PTSD wins, we all lose, including our family. So take a moment so that you can see the ripple effect, then ask yourself now far or wide will this enemy have to travel within your family before you bring it to a stop? I love you and want you to stay alive not only for yourself but for the many other people in your life who love you and want you to know it. Now with your emotions being taken by this enemy, your loved ones don't know how to come to you with their love and affection, and with the help of this enemy it aid us in pushing them away. So if you remember nothing else, remember that we do love you and always will.

The mind is a terrible thing to waste, so don't let it die. This enemy works on the mind and is trying hard to take us out. This enemy can either work against us or for us. On the one side of that coin, is the new information that you can use to tell ourselves the truth that you do need help. Now for me there was a time when my mind told me that there was a boogey-man under the bed. I went looking for him, and with that one belief, it kept me from going out into the world and enjoying my life or my family's lives. When this enemy beguns to take life away from me, it stop me from thinking about myself and what was really going on with me, I for one really believed that it was going on only from the outside and whatever happened in those traumas was my fault in some kind of crazy way. This enemy also wouldn't let me see or believe that I needed help from anyone. When others would tell me to take a look at myself, I thought that they didn't mean me any good, so I stayed away from them. Here's where I hope that you will stop listening to this enemy and start listening to what I am saying to you with these words. Ask yourself one question right now: Where is the answer to these question coming from your mind or the enemy within my mind? With that one answer you will know who is up there and what it's trying to do now that you are trying to seek some help for yourself . This won't be very hard if the enemy is alive and well within; however, if you can't see the similarity here, please don't look for differences to rule this out. Knowing what can happen to any animal that runs within a herd, sheep, goat, or people, when one leaves the herd, they get eaten by the wolf, PTSD, by traveling alone. So stay with me here and don't let the differences stop you from going forward on this journey or looking at the many ways that this enemy job is working on taking life, not giving life. I know that these can be some new views or ways to see this enemy, but if you want jump the gun here you can become one of the few who will survive this enemy and learn something that will save your life, along with many others headed down this road.

Saving your life will save many other lives from all walks of life that have slept or will sleep with this enemy. I know you might not be able to see it from where you are now, but believe me, it will. You see, long as there are wars, abuse, rape, and children dying in ways that we don't want to talk about, there will be this enemy from within that sleeps with many and is out to take your life. This is so you won't tell yourself those same old lies like others did before you, that this enemy isn't alive or won't take your lives. But we know from deep within ourselves that it is alive and will take lives—yours or someone you know who is living and fighting with this enemy right now. If you won't say so, then I will because it's still a life-or-death battle for me today, even after learning something about this enemy. There are days I still must get up and go out and find some reason not to let this enemy win, after years of it telling me that my life doesn't mean anything to anyone or my family. Once you have had any kind of trauma, there will always be relapses that come from your mind with thoughts like it's your fault for whatever took place within that trauma. You may relapse when you go by certain places or touch something or taste something, or from the smell of something that helps you remember what happened to you or to a person or thing that you cared for or loved—even from some of those events where you were the victim. So you see, this enemy has many ways to get into one's head. One of these ways involves people who have been traumatized and take on a label—that's right, when our society starts pointing fingers with name calling, it sends negative messages that send us into hiding, where this enemy can gets us alone. One of those labels that comes to mind is "mentally ill." That one has sent many to places where this enemy can and did take lives. So don't read this chapter in hopes that you will find differences; instead, see it for what it really is: hope. From within this chapter there will be new views and solutions for anyone who wants help or wants to help their loved one who is sleeping with this enemy. I hope this will help them see what this enemy is taking from their lives, so let's get to work by trying to save as many as we can. If you can save just one, hopefully that one is you.

There are many ways that the body can die. Without killing the physical body, this enemy will try to kill it off piece by piece, by driving us to do things to the body a little at a time. I started doing things to my body that I didn't think would hurt anyone but me. That was a big mistake, you see, not knowing or understanding the ways those things could kill me slowly. When I talk about slowly, yes, I'm talking about some of the three things I have already talked about in this chapter and then some. The human body is made up of many parts, but I believe that there are four parts that are very important. So let's take a deeper look at how abusing these parts almost sent me to my grave.

The enemy first started in on my body with my spirit, mind, and emotions confused and all over the place, sending me into denial that nothing was wrong with me. Then it sent me into isolation, put me in a place where the body wouldn't be around others. That meant staying inside all day and sometimes all night. I didn't think that was such a big deal at first, but let me tell you this about isolation. Most of the time when I was in isolation I was inside, out of the sunlight, not thinking that it would hurt me that much. Oh, how wrong I was. You see, the body needs the sunlight for energy to grow; without the sun we all start to die just a little every day. Most of all the body starts to lose some of its mobility. Believe me, some of these wounds help along the process of lifelessness. When we are in isolation there are many other parts of this enemy PTSD that begin to work, first by telling you things that we already talked about. That is, if you haven't fallen to sleep with this enemy while you were reading. For example, the enemy will tell you that you don't need anyone or any help from anyone, and you can do it alone. WRONG. Remember that it's out to kill the body and take life from us. Even at this point the body could seem helpless from isolation so you can't stay awake. When we stop being a part of life, we start to die from within, and those wounds can't be seen from the outside like the external wounds. So please don't isolate yourself and let this enemy get you alone, for there are many of your loved ones who need you and love you.

Now that you have an idea how this enemy can bring death to the body, let's look at some other ways that this will happen. There are always things like drugs and alcohol just to name two, so let's look at these. With drugs there are two kinds that you must be on the lookout for: first there are street drugs that we all say at one time or another that we won't get into, but with this enemy and isolation, anything is possible. Then there are the drugs that doctors give us to help with this enemy that many come to abuse.

I told myself that marijuana wouldn't hurt and that nothing

else would follow. Boy, was I wrong. You see, with all the other things going on with me from within, I couldn't see the harm that I was doing to my body. It started with paranoia, that someone was out to get me or watching me all the time. That meant I would stay away from others or look at them as someone who didn't like me or want anything to do with me. So with that first drug, the door opened for many others to follow; for me that was the beginning of a long life of drug abuse, so don't let this enemy tell you those same old lies. I know as we are speaking this enemy is probably telling you not to listen because it won't happen to you and trying to get you to look at your drug for the differences and not for the similarity. This enemy is out to kill you and it do not want to look for similarity,however, if you can you will have a great chance of stay alive, believe me here it's a fact.

For many years I ran from this by changing drugs, however sooner are later they all will tell us that same old lie that our life is worthless and that no one will miss us after we are gone. So it kept me trapped in that world so long that it was only by the grace of GOD and others who had been through those the drugs life that I was able to escape before this enemy took my life. Don't let this become you only because you won't take another look at this enemy as something that is out to take your life, not preserve it. From my experience people who try one drug most likely will try others. And with drugs being something that doctors use to treat the enemy, it makes it a little easier to get addicted. Not to say that medications won't help, because they do. If you have had a problem with drugs while sleeping with this enemy and it has started to take over your life, then this is something you need to be honest about with the doctor and people who you are reaching out to for help. I must tell you this because this enemy is so cunning and powerful that it will and can turn us against ourselves using our own best thinking. So please don't think for a minute that what I am saying is something to hurt you or make you feel any lesser of yourself; it's just that you are fighting for your lives here and nothing is off limits. So take a good long, hard look with me at those feelings and nightmares that have begun to take life from you a little at a time. Now some people won't tell you that alcohol is a drug, but it is one of the most used drugs for people who live with this enemy, one because it's socially acceptable and two, because it's a depressor. It is one of the drugs that this enemy uses and will tell you that it's not against the law; the other thing about this drug is that it numbs you.

All these things bring about a lot of things that will take life from us; they won't help us with staying alive from within and without, not to mention the guilt and shame that come along with the changes it does to the body or to our behavior, so please don't take this lightly. Just because you may not be aware of this enemy or can't see it, that's not to say it's not there or it's not trying to take over your life and eventually kill the body. We all know that death can be mental, physical, or spiritual. If you are lost in life, then take it from someone who was lost for many years; it's something that can be very hard and painful to come back from. For me it was the days that I went lost from my children, my wife, and my siblings.

Now some of these may not have anything to do with you or

maybe you are not in that place in life at this time. However, that's why I'm here so that you won't have to go through these with this enemy ALONE, to help you get out of your mind and back to living life. This may seem to be something out of a horror movie, but trust me, it is not.

Like I said before; there are many other ways that this enemy can attack the body. There were other ways that this enemy attacked my mind, being that I was in a war where most of my trauma happened. I was an adrenaline junkie, but for you it may be work or alcohol. That's right, some of us want to work all day and night to stay away from this enemy. That way we can tell ourselves that everything is all right, because doing it makes us seem well in the eyes of our public. But too much work takes a toll on the body, mind, and spirit. You see, there are so many ways and distractions that this enemy can use to come at you, and you will need some help from others to fight against this enemy that is out to take your life. Don't forget that we are here twenty-four hours a day and seven days a week, fighting along with you for our lives also.

With these things fresh on your mind and your heart, being full of life and love, let's do something about the enemy; first and foremost, don't let it take over any more pieces of you. Second, don't listen to the voice from within that is telling you it's all right not to call someone and tell them that you need help. If you can't find someone to call, look in the back of this book; there will be someone or someplace to call right now. We love you and they do too. (FAMILY)

CHAPTER 10

Being a Part of, Not Apart From

THERE ARE MANY places and groups that we have been a part of in our lifetime, they are a few I believe we need— to take a long and hard look at before you separate yourself from them. This was a question that I found that I needed to ask self after sleeping with this enemy. For myself far along time I found many reason to. For me, it's our society first then came my family,and so let's take a look at both them from my point of view after living some time with this enemy and learning many lessons from both sides of the coin. One side of the coin being our society part, that when you refuse to get help from the very people in society who have traveled down this road or have knowledge of this enemy. For when you do, you become like a person on an island all alone. By doing that it puts your family at risk of not knowing how to help us or themselves with this enemy that will attack them as well as you. You see, when

I thought that I could go this alone, I opened the door for this enemy to run wild not only with me, but also with other in my family. So don't be one of those who becomes apart from us, because we need you as much as you need us. This enemy is growing with the same information that we learn about it as we do because it lives within us. Now that may not sound right, but if you just think back from the time you started reading this book until now, you will see how much you have learned and how the enemy is trying to stop you from looking at ways you can help yourself and other in life. Most of all you stop being afraid and begun to see the freedom for yourself and how you may help other on their journey to freedom.

This is just one of the way of, *being apart from,* that this enemy is trying to get you alone. Also by keeping you from the society of men and women who slept with this enemy so that it can tell you what you can or can not do. Here is another one that I think will help you to look at the enemy a little closer.

When I first heard about this enemy that others were sleeping with, the first thing I did was run, Being a part of that group what I thought was that we all was crazy, people who had lost their minds. Oh, little did I know that making this apart of my thinking that it would hurt me in the long run. By being a part of that group, thinking the way that group of people through and using that way to find answer for my problem, let this enemy(PTSD) with me longer. By being *apart from the right people* I didn't get the right information to fight this enemy or give it to my family a fighting chance before it begin sleeping with them. Not only that, it took me to many of those places we talk about in this book earlier, with that group and society not having any new information about this enemy. By being a part of that society that let other go on this journey alone, with no new information to warn them beforehand it help me to get to some of those placer sooner. So there, if you still don't believe that being apart from us can't hurt you in the long run, think again; it can and will do these things to you and as many of your family members as it can. So don't be hardheaded here; don't let this separate you from us any longer than it already has. We love you and need you on this battlefield to fight with us, not on your own.

Now that you have some idea about that side of the coin, let's you and I look at the other side together about being *a part of* and what I found out on this journey of mine. You see, you can be connected to a source who are people who have slept with this enemy and are willing to share some of the things that worked for them, and I found that being a part of something that is helpful was bad after all. There are many ways to be connected to this source: one was with the doctor who had the right information and medication to help you not only to survive, but also so that we could help our family stay alive and well while dealing with me and this enemy. The other was getting with people who were willing to tell their stories about this enemy, how it lived and grew from within you. The first thing I had to believe that these people weren't the ones out to put me away in some of those dark places I have already talked about in this book. Be connected to the right information and believe the people that it came from. If you are to be a part of us, you must know from within that you not alone and there is an enemy that is out to take your life and the lives of your loved ones.

Hearing this may make you somewhat afraid of what others might think about you but listen to me right here and right now. That's not your thinking; it's coming from the enemy that lives within you. We all know that in life we will always be a part of something whether it's for life or death, so you make the call—which do you want here. Being a part of us, you will be fighting for your life and the lives of your family and mankind, most of all for your future and your children's future. If you don't have any at this time, then the future of many others who may have lost the fight to this enemy the taker of life. So please choose with your heart if your mind is being run by this enemy from within.

Now I'm going to leave this chapter because you may remember I said that I won't leave you in a dark place with your thoughts alone. The fight is not yours alone but all of ours who are praying that you will stay *a part of* and not run and be *apart from*. We love you and will never leave anyone behind.

CHAPTER 11

Wake Up (Your Life Is Waiting on You)

WHEN YOU FIND out that helping others is a part of our journey in life, we will then know for yourself that we are a survivor, not a victim. There were many things on this journey that help you find your way, however there maybe many other that you maybe still having trouble with. I want you to just keep your head up and let's do something that we all need to do every once in a while, and that is to go back through our journey.

You see, there was a time when I thought there was no way out. Not so. That was when this enemy didn't have a name and people wanted to put me away into one of those dark places where I sat and let others write my life story. But for me and many others, that same old lie is no longer truth.

This is something that I'm telling you from my truth and

maybe it's yours, if you are at home with yourself, or willing to go back through this book to find some of those places that you readed or saw some of your truth for yourself that was there just waiting for to wake up. The good news is that right here in this moment where you and I are on a journey, we are beginning to grow as long as we do the things to stay above ground, and yes you, too, will survive. On this journey there will be many valleys and hills and all of them for me were lessons in life that were created just for me and only me. You see, there was one thing I had to do first for myself, and that was to stop listening to the people who were saying that I could not, and listening to the others who were saying that they did and so could I. Most of all I had to find someone or something that I could believe in, for me at first, they were people who had slept with this enemy and no matter what had stayed alive to tell their story to doctors and others who would listen to them. Getting that new information started a new belief along with a overhaul, it changed my whole belief system. Then I thought what I was going through was just for me, but today I know it was for others who would come after me. So you see there is a part of your journey that you weren't the only one created for it, and the good news is that you have what it takes from within to walk through whatever this enemy threw at you. There is a saying in another belief system of mine and many other belief systems that says we all have a cross to bear. However, from this cross it can be one of the best crosses that you will ever carry from it you may find —some peace and love for yourself and mankind. So let's get to work on this journey and receive some healing and growth within the mind. I'm still on my journey of healing from this enemy that I have slept with for years just to get here. I'm hoping writing this will help you and me to get a higher level of our healing in life. Also, with some help from me and others you can write your own next chapter in our lives, with faith that many others will follow. Now let me tell a little about how I changed my belief system about this enemy.

I started to look at these valleys like a classroom full of lessons for me to get to the next level in life. You see why I call them the classroom of life. Well, from what I learned in a book I wrote, *Looking at You, Finding Myself,* there are many classrooms in what I found to be Earth's school of life, where they was given to us in life by the creator of life. I believe today. In that book I found ways to change many of my belief systems that were given to me from others who didn't have any experience, knowledge, or information about PTSD.

Knowing that someone else has gone through what you are going through can be one of the best gifts you can receive in life. So you see it would be just about impossible for us to help each other unless there was someone who had either opened the door for us or turned on the light in the dark. Now there is another way to look at this changing of belief systems, so let's look at that change in another way. In many of these classrooms in Earth's school of life, I learned to be grateful to others and, what I can now say to you, for all that we have talked about in this book. Be grateful for that time you spend in your valley; review some of those times and try hard to look at some of those people who were in those valleys with you and be able to finding yourself. There you will truly find some of your greatest gifts in life, and just maybe you will find something in one of them that will help you get out of the space you are in. Your life is truly waiting on you, so get up and go out there and get to work on living, not waiting for your death.

There will be times on this journey with this enemy that we sleep with when it may seem like there is no life for you, but if you will take a little time and look at some of my journey and see where I am now, you will know that your life is waiting on you too. I was at that place many times on my journey, before I had those lessons in Earth's classes of life. I found that some of those places on my journey were *my meantime* in life. You may be at one of those crossroads now, where you can go right or left, forward or backward. Right there is where you will find that place in life that I call *in the meantime*. This is what I was talking about when I told you that someone or something will bring the light of life to you, myself or others who have slept with this enemy from within. What I want you to know is it's all right to be afraid or to feel that you are stuck—for that, my friend, is the meantime of life. Here's where others have let fear stop them from getting a hand up, not a handout. For me, this place came many times on my journey, but I had many others to call to that help me fight a good fight. I made it through, my friend, so can you. Now don't give up or out, just sit awhile with me here, so that these lessons that have come to me from the many battles with this enemy PTSD will aid you on your journey also.

Let's see if I can help you with a few of those battles. This fight helped me and others survive, and we are here today with a voice and a light of hope. You are not alone, there are many others, and we won't let them fall in the cracks of life. We won't let your dreams go to waste that you had not only for yourself but for other loved ones. The hope that will help them stand and be proud of the time that life put you through and saw you come out the other side, with more love for THEM and many others who still sleep with that enemy called PTSD. So, are you with me here, ready to see what life may be calling you to do with your glory? There is a saying that we are given many parts to play in life,and so you can see from these many classrooms in Earth's school of life. Millions will have to endure so no one is left behind, to help mankind become the greatest human race it can be. So will you be one of the ones who will be willing to helps take mankind its next level with information about this enemy with your story? Believe me here your story could give our society something to help other on their journey, not just one but many that don't believe that what they was put on this earth for in the first place help other. There were many times on this journey sleeping with this enemy I thought that I wasn't going to make it, and try very hard not hearing that voice that now I hope you can hear from our little time together. That will help us fight the good fight and to find other to give them new information about this enemy. I saw and believed for myself that I did have a life and that it was worth fighting for. Now I hope you will accept this from me and others who will love us until we can love ourselves. There were times I wanted to die or tried to kill myself, but after listening to others who had fought with this enemy that we sleep with, PTSD, I found the strength and the courage to stay alive, I know you will too. So hear me, my fellow soldier in this war against this enemy, there are still many out there crying out for help. If you can't hear your life calling you or see that it is waiting on you, then I'll be the voice here calling to you and telling you that your life is waiting on you. Hopefully by telling you some of my history with this enemy that I slept with for years, you will know that your life is calling. I hope that my stories of hope will do for you what many other stories and tears on this journey with this enemy, PTSD, did for ME. There is one thing for sure; they kept me alive and fighting for my life until I heard the right voice or the right story that gave me the strength and courage to fight for my life and to tell my story. I won't sit here and tell you stories about PTSD that will have you think that this enemy is going to sit there and take this fight without a fight because that would be a lie. However, I will take the time to draw you a picture of this enemy that says you can beat it, find your way not only to the life that is waiting on you but home to your loved ones. Most of all you'll have the strength and courage to help many others who still sleep with the enemy, which is not only out to rob your life but your love's one life also. There will be many who like you to believe that there is no hope, or they don't really care about people who sleep with this enemy, PTSD. I'm not one of them because I know that this enemy can be beaten and with that beating it can and will help the mental health field. Our society likes to label people, places, and things as good or bad, but most of all they like to play the blame game when something goes wrong. Many of them are afraid to face the truth, not because of the truth, but due to what is going on in their life with this enemy that may be running loose in their family. Not because of what they know but from what they were told. So don't just sit there listening to them and let your life pass you by; instead, try hearing the call from life saying, "Hey, you there, I'm waiting for you. Come on!"

You may or may not hear your life calling as of yet, but my hope is that you may have read something that may help you begin to fight and that you won't let our society drown out that voice that stops you from fighting for the life that you were created for from the beginning of time. This is an enemy that I have been living with and fighting with for some time now, but with that fight and with the help of others I have reclaimed many parts of life, with a place in this society. I no longer just sit and cry or feel sorry for myself; I won't give up my fight with this enemy PTSD, not only because I have a cross to carry but also the cross I carry for others who want to be free from this enemy. So please don't sit there—get out and go out there and show the world and our society that you are a survivor.

CHAPTER 12

Coming Out of Darkness into the Light (Healing)

THIS IS A chapter you will find yourself coming back to read over and over, so read it carefully, I hope that you can find some love for yourself right where you on your journey when you do. Why? I believe from my experience that we will have to come from many dark places to the light on our journey in life. Not that dark places are all bad or good; it's just that the healing process takes on many changes and from many points of view. You see, after getting new information about this enemy that I slept with for those years, I found myself not only believing but seeing this enemy for myself. There were places that I didn't know were dark places in my life at the time. Those are some of the places where I'm going try to bring some light to here and now, but there was another place that I didn't know about and couldn't see at the time, and I wouldn't let anyone else bring the light into my life at that time. That's why it's important for me to get right down to work with this information and hope you find the light in some of your dark places in life.

This enemy that sleeps within us is learning as we learn each day, and I will try my best to bring the light, with hope that it won't send me back into the darkness. There are dark places in everyone's life where we can run and hide, where no one will know or see our fear, or know anything about the enemy that we are running from or living with. That way we can pretend we don't care about what others might think about us. The truth is that most of them wanted to put us away or stop loving us altogether, so right here and now I will bring you the light in that darkness by saying that many of us who slept with this enemy have found some peace for ourselves. Meanwhile I want you to know that I love you and will always keep the light on for you and for the many others who will need it. Until we all find some freedom from this enemy that lives within, none of us will be free; the truth is that no one free is until we all are free.

There were many other hiding places that we talked about on this journey, so by now you could know some of these dark places in your life that you have read about up until now from the outside; however, there are many other places that you will have taken a look at from the within where this enemy not only lives but also is learning more about us. One thing I have learned about this enemy that we sleep with is that it is learning whatever— we are learning about it along with the new knowledge and information that is being given from others. One of those dark places I will talk about first is self-hate. No matter how much this enemy comes at you with it, you can always stop him cold in his tracks with self-love. So, this is one place where you must try your best to keep an open mind too, not what others, are doing to you with that hate but what you are doing to yourself.

There may be a lot of other things going on with you at this time but the one that I'm most worried about is your self-love; without letting some light in that dark place, this enemy will keep you on the run from the truth and the right information that some of the people who have been through it can and will share it with you. Now on your journey so far you may have heard that this enemy is nothing more than a figment of your imagination. However, with this information you don't have to let them keep you in that place in life anymore; you don't have to let it keep you from showing up and giving this world the many gifts that God and only God gave you. That can bring help to this world to combat this enemy(PTSD) and to help others find their higher selves.

This is one those things about this enemy that we can all find in common, those who sleep with it now and those who slept with it in the past. If not it may keep us in this dark place from some of our trauma. You may have gone through this dark place or are going through it at this time. I don't want you to let this enemy, PTSD, take you deeper into that hole in your life, so you won't want to come out. Most importantly I want you to let someone in. Hold on to the light, for we are all fighting this enemy that lives within us. We will use all that we learned to bring you home, not only for your family but also for yourself so that you will become a fighter against this enemy with others.

I know we all have our own beliefs about a higher power, and to me this higher power is the LORD GOD, JESUS CHIRIST, my savior and lord. Now hold on there—I am not trying to take you down a road of religion. I am only trying to open a door with that statement to say that we as human beings need something greater and higher then self in our lives. Why? Because I believe that every human being needs something to trust, something larger than man, and I believe it must come from within. This again is a stronghold that PTSD doesn't want us to find or bring light to. It doesn't want us to find hope or to believe in ourselves. I learned from many years fighting and sleeping with this enemy that I had to find a higher power when it was just me and PTSD, when I couldn't go to anyone or call to anyone. That higher power that I call the Lord thy God (Jesus Christ), that would comfort me so that I wouldn't take my life or hurt other and helped me make it through those times. But to find someone that he had already sent through those storms who had fought this enemy and made it to the other side to keep the light on for me, so you see, this is a dark place that you are running from not too. All because of that enemy that we sleep with from within wants us to give up; not to do the work we need to do or help others. We need to keep the light on for others to make sure that on their journey there will be a light on for them and for those still in darkest.

On this journey I learned that you have to find your authentic self. That's right, the person was created for that trauma, that happen to you just for you and only you. What I mean by your authentic self is the person that you are, so you will know your purpose on this journey with that trauma, from your finding of your authentic self from within you will know the truth, which is you was created for this problem to help other. From within every trauma and each person from their trauma it is to aid them in take a good look within. From looking within at this stage of the journey, you will find your truth from within yourself where you found your authentic self, that whatever in life that we go through it's to help other. Now you know some truth with that truth my hope is that you will found out that your life is waiting on you, so get up and take back your life with your authentic self.

Don't forget that when you are in your darkest moment, there is still a light at the end of the tunnel, but when you find yourself in some of your longest days and sleepless nights, there is always a light from within. Know that you were created for this time and place, and for this enemy that is out not only to take your life but the lives of many others who have not learned what you are learning. Or better yet what you are reading now, so pass it on, for none of us are free until we all are free.

Now you need to do what others have done when they come to a new lesson or a blessing—get up from there and put it into action what you have read! Yes, you, get up from there and take back your loved ones and bring to the world what you were created to do, help with the healing process in life that we all try to do , and take your place in history, for you are one of the many, not the few, who sleep with this enemy, PTSD, from within.

The light is on and we are waiting, so come on out of your darkness to your glory.

Now, how far can you see?

CHAPTER 13

PTSD, A Mental Illness Issue (It's Not a Disease; It's a Sickness)

THERE ARE MANY who would want you to believe that this illness is a disease, but I want you to know from the very beginning that it is a mental illness that can come from some trauma that we may have in life. Mine happens to come from the Vietnam War, mostly from some of the trauma that I went through in that war. But there are many other traumas that can bring on this illness.

Many years ago before many in the medical field got new information in the mental health field, many in that field diagnose war veterans as beinged shellshock other that had traumas with other illness . However, some doctors who didn't want to hold on to the old beliefs and a few Vietnam veterans took on the medical field and set out to change that belief for our society so that they wouldn't look at us like we had a disease and had to be locked away, or believe that we couldn't do anything or had to be medicate. So I'm here to let you know that that lie will not be tolerated anymore by myself or by the others who have slept with that enemy. What I hope to do is to shine some light on this enemy that I have come to know as PTSD, so sit up and open the door to life and let in the love from myself and others, so that you won't have listen to those people who say you are not worthy. This will take a lot of work from all of us, I am counting you to become one in this fight, fighting for your life and the lives of many others that we lost along the way. You see, now that you have found some new information about this enemy and our society, you don't have to be alone, waiting on life; you can go out and start a new chapter in your book of life.

Being mentally ill is not a life sentence where you have to sit around letting others control your life; it is something that we can learn and grow with, which will not only help you but many others who are just finding out about PTSD. Whoever they are, they can get help from the mental health field. Knowing the name of an enemy that you sleep with, PTSD, can be good news, so you no longer have to sit around with the blinds pulled down, running away from life, now you can run to it.

There is another thing I want you to take a good look at and that is who and where you getting your information from about this enemy that you are sleeping or living with day in and day out. From my experience this enemy has as many faces and ways to affect us or to show up in our lives. I want you to always keep in mind the different ways this enemy will find ways to help you disqualify yourself from what you are doing to yourself. So as we have learned just from our own experience, there are some liars out there, and there are many lies that you may have told yourself. However, I don't want you to stop seeking professional help, because there are many people now with some good information about this mental illness. There are many other books that have been written about this enemy. Which one is the right one for you? That is something you are going to have to find out for yourself; you will have to do some work, but you don't have to do it alone if you don't want to. We know that finding the right information that addresses this enemy can be the best way to combat(PTSD). Remember, you are never alone or without help; we are here with you to fight the good fight to help you stay alive. Also to keep sending out new information about this enemy just as long as we all take a stand. What I have found is not to let others hold you back from finding the truth about this enemy and your life, not even our own family members or society. These are some harsh words, but I believe that they need to be said, yes, because we do need to hear them. I pray that you take them to heart because our family and society really don't have an idea what we are up against. Most of them don't even know what to call this enemy, not to say anything about what mental illness is itself. So remember, this is your fight, but you are not alone or without others who have been there, done that, got the T-shirt.

This is not a long chapter but one with a message that will help you see through the fog and some of the lies from others, in hope that you can find some truth for yourselves. Now even if you must read this chapter many times, don't let the words from these pages find you sitting in that dark room again talking to yourself. This sickness is something that you can live a healthy life with. It's just like any other sickness. One thing for sure, there are people out here with the help you need for yourself and your love ones if they want it. Ask yourself why you're still reading this book. Better yet, why did this book call out to you and so many others who sleep with this enemy? I have more good news to help you along the way. The good news is that your spirit and your soul will hear it and feel good for the first time in a long time, because of that small voice that we all hear sometimes and refuse to listen to. Well, now that you do, thank you for coming aboard; thank you for listening to it and doing what your spirit is asking of you.

I'm going to have to leave this chapter here; there are many other things I would like to talk about before I bring this book to a close. The world is waiting on it, and our brothers and sisters are in some of those places being told that same old lie about this mental illness. One thing more than any other thing that bothers me is that some of our brothers and sisters are being put in places because of this enemy that is now known as PTSD. Some of them have slept with this enemy for many years without knowing what or where to find help with this illness. Others before now had to go it alone; now all we have to do is take a stand and fight back. This can be done by doing the work we need to do on ourselves, learning all we can about this enemy, and getting the proper help from the right people. Many others will sleep with it before they find some peace from their many eternal wounds; life itself has its own way of taking people through some trauma, whether it's losing one of our loved ones or going through the ups and downs in life. So remember, you don't have a disease. The next time someone wants to know about PTSD and you're not sure, don't let them give you answers from what they heard or from other people who haven't lived with this enemy tell you.

You see, living and sleeping with Post-Traumatic Stress Disorder is durable, most of all you can do it too. The most important thing is that you have to know in your heart of heart that you, too, can become a leading civilian in our society, so hold on to your seat. I still have a lot to talk about.

CHAPTER 14

Until It Happens to You

THERE IS ONE thing I want you to know for sure and that is until something happens to you, the only thing you can say is what you think you would do or what others said they did that don't have an idea of what you deal with. So until it happens to you, don't go around saying what you heard along the way that others did. With this enemy many think that what we are going through is something that we can just get over or let go. Well, I'm here to tell you and your loved ones this—it's not that simple. You see, PTSD attacks people in many different forms,. I throught I could do just that get over it, but there is another side to this story and another side of this enemy that just doesn't let you go in one day or one year. I will try my best to help you hear some of the things that people who never slept with this enemy say to me. In my life in hopes that you won't have to go there, or if you do, you won't stay there as long as I did. Like my mother always said, there are two sides to a coin, it depends on what side of the coin you looking at. Now, in your case you will have to know what side of this enemy you can see in your life today. Let me put it a little more directly so you can decide for yourself in what ways you are sleeping with this enemy.

PTSD (Post-Traumatic Stress Disorder) has now come full circle as a mental illness. This is something that is not just becoming a part of our society but has been with us for a very long time. For years doctors and family members didn't know what to call it. I won't get into that same old blame game that others played before us. Our lives are at stake here, along with many others who are being put away as I'm writing this book. I don't have the time or energy to put in that blame game after all these years and knowing some what I do now. I'm still sleeping with this enemy and he is still trying to take my life, he is also trying keep me away from my family and society. So stay with me here so that you won't become one of this enemy's victims.

As you know, with this enemy comes stigma that can hurt you in our society, from the person who sees this on your job appreciation to the doctor who sees it on your health record. They will put you in a category from what they heard or read about someone else who didn't get the proper help or the tools to fight against this enemy. What this can to do a person is give them a life sentence with this illness, that tell other what you can't do, and help you tell yourself only what you can look forward to in your future. Hopefully you have an idea where I am going with this, so let's get down to some real talk. You see, when I first came back from that war, I was told that I was shell-edshocked and was put in our society to fight this enemy with the information from that point view. Then others started to have the same problem I did. One of the first things that this enemy took away from me was my family. I couldn't be around them when they were having a get-together, and that started to isolate me from everyone. It put me in a very lonely and dark place in life; from there I did a lot of harm to myself. With isolation, I let the enemy take me deep into what I know now as depression, anger, and resentment. I thought that my family should have been the very people to understand what I was going through, but PTSD feeds on the mind, also with your family member.. This is one of the ways it works on you when you have been traumatized from one thing or another. One thing for sure is that I didn't want others to know how badly or what I was hurting from. Trauma can and do happen in life, they could be something that happen to you and you are reliving that event over and over, day or night when you are alone, triggered from a smell or sound. You may have some kind of flashback from them throughout the day. Now some of these traumas came from what I personally went through and others from what I saw happen to some of my friends. Here is the funny part: I had heard others talk about what happened to them, but when it came my time, I fought hard and long to keep it to myself. I now know that was one of the first mistakes I made with this enemy. You see, if no one knows what's going on with you, then how can they help you? This just gives the enemy time to take me for what I call a long ride.

At first, I didn't believe that I was doing all the things that my loved ones were telling me I was doing, like sitting alone in my room crying all the time, or wetting the bed at night from nightmares. Now you've got to remember I was one of those big bad Vietnam War heroes; I wasn't about to say anything about those things. And then one night the enemy woke me up from a nightmare and the bed was wet from me being afraid of the dark. Not to say anything about the time I broke out running from what I thought was gunfire, just to find out it was only a car backfiring. These are just a few of the many ways that this enemy called PTSD had me fighting the world and thinking that everyone and everything around me was in some way trying to take me out.

When there is a trauma in your life, Post-Traumatic Stress Disorder can lead you toward some of those places I talk about early in this book. Most of all it made me believe that my loved ones couldn't be trusted with my secret or I couldn't be around them. I prayed that they would get to know anything about what was going on within me. This enemy was talking to me in my head, saying that they would not like it if they knew the truth about me, so I ran from them too.

Don't let what happened in someone else's life stop you from finding some of the help I talk about. Learn as much about PTSD for yourself or from a knowledgeable doctor before this enemy takes you down that long road that I had to travel without help and not knowing anything about PTSD. Will you do that for me and the rest of those who are on this journey seeking help? Try your best to learn from others who have found help and find out where the help came from.

With this enemy there will be many new faces; it's an illness that affects each person in different ways. There are people trying to find new ways to treat PTSD, and I hope that you have an idea about how this enemy or illness works on people so you won't have to be a test tube for those who are trying to call it something else.

There is nothing that will happen to you that you can't handle with this enemy. I know, believe me here. Now from the unknowing there will be some fear, but I will be there with you all the way. All you have to do is keep me close to you with some of these words in this book like a prayer, and in your heart with some of what I did and continue to do to this day to stay alive.

This enemy is real, it is out to take you away from all that you can be and from all the people you love the most. If you don't want your life to be run by others or this enemy, here's what I suggest you try. When this enemy begins to tell you things like your life doesn't mean anything or you are not worth anything to this world, you must tell it that it's a liar. This may not seem real to you, but until this happens to you, you're going to have to make up your mind for yourself or find some truth somewhere in your heart. Are you in trouble? If so, then please for me and yourself start doing something about your PTSD, if you one of us,or you will go into hiding for years like myself and other did. Trust me on this.

Are your family beginnig to stay away from you like some of mind did,beginning to think that those things that other was saying about you was true,like you are crazy or going crazy, and after a while this enemy started telling me the same thing, so I went into isolation from my family and the world around me. Then I started to let this enemy tell me when to come out, where to go, and who to talk to, like only other that they call crazy too, not knowing whether they were sleeping with this enemy or something else was going on with them—I didn't care. What I really wanted was someone who looked like me and thought like me. What I'm trying to say here is that until it happens to you, these things may seem far from your mind, so be on the look out for them from outside and from within self.

One thing about this enemy is that he sleeps with people who have been traumatized from far less trauma than I had. You see, the cause and the effect from trauma can come from many things that we go through in life, so don't let anyone tell you first and foremost that PTSD is not real. They will tell you that this is one of those things that people will go through in life, so get over it. Some can, many can't. I just want you to know that we are out here and will go through it with you. So hold on, we're coming for you. If nothing else my military life taught me that we will never leave anyone behind in the war zone, and we are in a war zone with this enemy. Now that you know you don't have to go through what you are going through, start here by getting some help—if not from the places I told you about in this book, then get some help from a support group or people who have gone through or going through what you are going through. By now you have to know that you are not alone; from this day forward, you never have to be alone again. So remember, this is not a disease but an illness, a mental health issue that can be helped with the right people or doctors, so come on, get out of those dark rooms or hiding places that you or someone else you know might be locked in and take back your life and your future—if not for yourself then for those people who need to hear your story. Your loved ones need you in their life, like your mother, father, and your children. They love you and so do I.

ARE YOU READY?

CHAPTER 15

Freedom Isn't Free

MANY ON THIS journey of ours believe that freedom is free. This is one of the things I need to talk about before I bring this work that we are doing together to a close. My PTSD is from what I have seen in life, just maybe from some of these things that you have read in this book, you will know that this enemy is out to take us out, in many ways. This is, my believe, something you need to know about because it's my hope that you will get it right from the very beginning: our freedom will not come free of charge.

You might be asking yourself, "What is the price for my freedom?" and for me it was any and everything that I could find to read also anywhere I could find others who had fought with this enemy and were willing to help me come out of the darkness into the light. That told me that I was somebody and my life did matter to them and others. I am telling you this in hopes that you won't stop fighting until you can find some peace in your life from this enemy called (PTSD) and won't let this society or anyone tell you that you are not worth the price, not taking no for an answer when all seems lost. So please don't stop looking for others who are telling their story. Are you telling your story to others who are still in some of those same dark places being told from those same old lies, that with this mental illness there is no help? Now you know there is help if you are willing to pay this price for yourself freedom and freedom for your loved ones, who are waiting with open arms with love and joy in their hearts and many prayers on their lips. I'm calling out to mothers, fathers, brothers, and sisters who are putting up a good fight to reclaim our lives. So, try to remember what I said that I to remember when I didn't know anything: I still had hope that someday someone would bring this enemy (PTSD) out of the darkness to the light so that our society wouldn't think that we were crazy, leaving us out of their neighborhood or school, not to mention the community.

Being in the military, I will leave no man behind. I will find you and bring you out if it's just with these words. I will do my best to bring you home safe, and I will not stop telling my story about how I fought a good fight with this enemy, with hope that you will pick your battleground and continue this fight. One day you will bring the light of truth about this enemy to others, so that they won't be sent to those dark rooms in life.

There are many forms of freedom but there has always been a price we had to pay, whether it be for people, places, or things. I fought in a war for people, places, and things so that they could have their freedom, and what I know is that it cost me and others dearly. So, don't rest easier here because whenever you have to go into battle, there are always going to be some wounds that come from other bravery. That's why I'm saying that freedom isn't free. Are you willing to fight for your freedom from this enemy known as (PTSD), knowing that there will be a lot of letting go of people, places, and things along with some of this society? This enemy is real, and this fight is for your life,and also for your freedom.

You see, the fight that I had to win first was believing that what was happening to me was real, not just something others told me to get over. Then there was the fight of not taking no for an answer and being told you can't win so don't try. These are some of the little battles I had to win with myself before I could get out of those rabbit holes, before I got to that places of no return, like drinking, drugging, or just isolating. Looking back now I can see these were part of this enemy's makeup; it wanted to kill me or keep me in pain by hurting myself with other destructive behavior.

We know that self-hate is not in our makeup as human being. So, with the little freedom that you have or are willing to get, you have already paid some kind of price are paying the price. Find the right help or the right path that will leads you up and out of your rabbit hole to the light of faith, hope, and GOD. I knew God was there with me through some of those long nights and days, and I called on him when there was no one else. Now don't run from me here; just sit with yourself with your thoughts to see if this is true or false. Did you call to someone or something from that rabbit hole? Let's keep it real here; there is someone we all call to and it's not another human being but a spiritual being. I knew that it would never have put me in some of those places that humans put me in or called me some of the names they called me. So, with that said and a victory behind us somewhat, let's get on to another battle and find even more freedom from this enemy, (PTSD) that we have slept with far too long and for way too many nights. Are you with me?

There is another place in our lives that I call strongholds, from which we must get freedom before any progress can be made. These are self-hate and self-talk. That's right, we must start loving ourselves, no matter where we are or whatever we're being told by others. You see, there comes a time when you know what others are saying about you and you don't feel right and your subconscious lets you believe what you're hearing from the outside, truly not who you are. Until you stop doing or listening to these things, freedom becomes no more than something you talk about or believe is just for others. I'm not saying never to listen to others, but sometimes you may want to listen with to your spirit from within; let it lead you to listen to other who starts their conversation off by saying, "Let me tell you what happened to me when I was in that place and how I got through that time in my life."

I'm not talking about a few here because there are many more that will help you find freedom and a life worth living again if you are willing to go to war with this enemy that I have come to know as (PTSD).

There are situations and circumstances we go through all the time in life, and there are some that come by just living life on life's terms. This might or might not be your situation, but if you are having any of these effects going on in your life, I would suggest that you take a long, hard look at it. Not because I said so but because there may be some of the causes and effects that went on with you that let this enemy in your life, or will let him in. Now these are just a few things that may help you find some freedom from (PTSD); they may also help keep this enemy out of your life or help you to understand that sleeping with this enemy may have helped him to sleep in other's lives who are close to you. Now don't just sit there and stay in that place; you now know you don't have to or want to. Having some of these causes and effects from any trauma and seeing what happened to others hopefully will cause you to run to self, not from self. So now with some self-love and a brighter view of your future, get out there and find some of that freedom that was given to you from the beginning of creation, that now has come from your knowing.

I don't believe you will let your life pass you by without a fight. So, get on with getting your life back and start having the future that I believe GOD, the creator of all mankind, intends for all his creation to have, and have it abundantly. With that said, I love you and I look forward to seeing you on the battlefield in this life against this enemy we have now come to know as (PTSD).

Conclusion

There are many ways that this enemy will come after you.trust me here. However, for those of you who have not yet come face-to-face with this enemy, here is some information that I pray that will help you start on road with your recovery from this enemy,(PTSD), also in hope that it will give you the courage to tell others that is suffering with this enemy that they in a fight for their very lives, so that people won't have to run from what they don't know about it anymore. Not only that so that other won't be thrown out into our society to defend for themselves or lock away somewhere. I know that there are many who are still sleeping with this enemy, that don't dare say anything about it to other because of some negative view that our society has about this enemy, however, I am here to tell you and others that this is a mental health issue which by now I hope you have found out for yourself. By now from your own truth, and know by now that there is help out there for people that have this problem, and hopefully you find some from what I talk about in this book or from other people who have slept with this enemy. By caring for themselves and sharing with you how they made it through some of their hard times, you will come to understand that may or may not have to go through some of those times, whenever and wherever they come up in our lives. Or should I say when this enemy decides to show his face in our lives.

There will always be those people who want look at us as bad people, but you need to know from the very beginning that you are not a bad person. You just may have spent too many nights and days with this enemy, (PTSD), that is out to take your life and your family hostages. By doing this it not only destroys your life but the lives of many. There is something about mental health that will always bring with it many causes and effects, and if we don't do anything about it, it can bring down a whole family. So, let's not lose sight of this enemy from within and run back to some of those hiding places I have told you about earlier in this book. If there is one thing that I learned on this journey from this enemy that I slept with for many of years,is that it's will let you think that it (PTSD) have left you alone and gone to sleep with someone else. Just long enough for you to stop doing one or two of the things that we talk about already in this book. First it will tell you to STOP SEEKING HELP and second to STOP TAKING MEDICATION. Please don't be fool by your feeling,those days when you are feeling better it will tell you stop doing the thing that got you to feel better in the first place.

This may or may not have helped you on your journey after coming through some of your trauma, but if it did then welcome to our world of healing, growing, and self-help. You need to know that most of this work you must do yourself, —I pray that you are up to it, because this is your life you're fighting for, and if you won't fight for your own life, then who do you think would do a better job? Now you have some insight of who and what (PTSD) looks like, tastes like, and hopefully feels like, so let's get to work because our tomorrow will be better than our today.

Your freedom is in your sight and you have some information fresh in your mind and heart. Don't give up the fight because the war is just beginning; this is one that we will win, if not for ourselves then for our loved ones that this enemy have kept us away from far too long, and most of all for that person who has fallen and doesn't have the strength or the courage to get up or fight for his or her life. You be the voice in the night that says, "I am here with open arms and love, with some peace for you; if you just take my hand, we will walk this journey together and find our freedom together."

Don't forget this enemy will trying like he has done in the past to get you off your journey of learning and putting up a good fight for your life. I will give you some footnotes to remember about him. First there can be some trauma that can let this enemy in your bed at night, then from some of those causes, from other things that I have talked about with you. War is where he came into my life from the beginning, but these are not the only ways he can enter your life, so don't rule yourself out. Domestic violence, or the death of smeone close to you, or maybe that child or person that may have die in your arms in car accident just to name a few, abuse, whether it be sexual or child abuse or spouse abuse, fire, flood, or just something that is traumatized to you, so let's not try to put too many names on it because then we may help others disqualify themselves from this enemy and be left in the dark, crying in the night, thinking that there is no way out. So, with that, remember that I love you and may GOD bless each one of you.

Thank You

Acknowledgment

First and foremost, I would like to thank my creator, my lord and savior Jesus Christ, who have brought me through this journey in life,and trusted me enough to be obeying in writing this book. There many others I would like to thank who aided me on this journey while I slept with this enemy, (PTSD). I still have days that I must get up and dress up to do battle with the enemy to make sure my children and grandchildren won't have to sleep with him. Nicole Gamble, Willie Gamble, and Reginald Gamble, who cheer me on from the sidelines, I thank you very much. To Louis Burns and Annie Lou Burns, who gave me a place to lay my head when I didn't have a place to go. —thank you and may God always bless you.

To all the veterans who give some and to the ones who give all, thank for your spirit support that kept me writing when I thought I didn't have the courage to stop the tears long enough to write another line. Thank you because you are the real heroes here.

Now to Audrey D. Gamble, who was my firstborn and probably slept with this enemy the longest, thank you for staying. To Alfonso Gamble Jr., thank you for loving from where you stood in life. Dad loves you, son, no matter what. Then there is Alfonso Lee, who loves me anyway after losing his mother and found it in his heart to forgive me for not being there with him during that time. Daddy will always love you and we will see your mother again, in our next life.

To the person who stuck with me when this enemy had me in the world of drugs and alcohol, not knowing if I wanted to live or die, Bertha Burns, honey, I love you. God is good all the time no matter where one may be in life. I pray that we will give thanks to him together on our remainder journey. I love you very much and God does too.

In closing I would like to thank all the doctors and nurses in the VA Hospital who helped me along the way and are still helping in this process of me getting to know this enemy (PTSD) that many still sleep with. I love you all and may God bless you all.

Thank you from the bottom of my heart.

Alfonso Gamble Sr.

CPSIA information can be obtained
at www.ICGtesting.com
Printed in the USA
FSHW022022021219
64615FS